Irène Lassus-

W9-AHA-806

111 Tastes of Paris That You Shouldn't Miss

Photographs by Julian Spalding

(111)

emons:

© Emons Verlag GmbH
All rights reserved
Photographs by Julian Spalding, except:
Karen Seiger (ch. 46 & ch. 100)
© Cover motif: depositphotos.com/VeraSimon
Layout: Eva Kraskes, based on a design
by Lübbeke | Naumann | Thoben
Edited by Rosalind Horton
Maps: altancicek.design, www.altancicek.de
Basic cartographical information from Openstreetmap,
© OpenStreetMap-Mitwirkende, ODbL
Printing and binding: Lensing Druck GmbH & Co. KG,
Feldbachacker 16, 44149 Dortmund
Printed in Germany 2019
ISBN 978-3-7408-0581-4
First edition

Did you enjoy it? Do you want more?
Join us in uncovering new places around the world on:
www.111places.com

Foreword

The French, and Parisians in particular, are perhaps the only people in the world who love talking about food while they're eating. They discuss not just what's on their plate but also what else they've been eating. 'So-and-so's goat's cheese, marinated herrings or ginger chocolates are to die for!' Half the time is spent exchanging addresses! I know many people (myself included) who are happy to cross Paris to buy an exceptional sourdough loaf or beef rib.

Traditional French cuisine is, of course, still the mainstay of the Parisian diet. But, increasingly, the city is attracting cooks and food retailers from around the world, inspired by the citizens' passion for eating. New places seem to open every morning, whether Italian, Japanese, South American or Scandinavian, and this doesn't include those that cater for special diets, such as vegetarian or vegan, with surprisingly tasty results.

Meeting the people behind these new enterprises has filled me with admiration. They put their hearts and souls into what is often very hard work. They're at once enthusiasts and experts. And all this with good humour, and lively imaginations, for many are inventing new combinations of tastes that are as delightful as they are surprising. A common factor is the quality of their ingredients, and the dedication of the farmers, fishermen and animal breeders who supply them deserves everyone's respect. This is the hidden mountain of effort on which the Capital of Gastronomy has been built.

Of course, TV food programmes have helped to generate this flowering of talents, but this is no bad thing given the threat that future generations face from the rise of junk food. My selection has, necessarily, been personal, and I ask the forgiveness of any I've overlooked. Perhaps a future edition will enable me to acknowledge burgeoning new talents in this ever-changing, vibrant scene.

111 Tastes

1 À la Mère de Famille

The oldest chocolate factory in Paris

Within a fabulous, ancient cut-glass and gilded setting, À la Mère de Famille offers an extraordinary range of over 1,200 different types of traditional sweets: chocolates, rochers pralines, Florentines, calissons, marshmallows, Bêtises de Cambrai, glacé fruits, pâtes de fruits, marrons glacés and liquorice. Among its treasures, found on a back shelf, are the roudoudou, a favourite of French children: a sweet of fruit-flavoured sugar paste served in a little seashell (they used to be real, but are now plastic). There are sweets for seasonal feasts and all special occasions – an army of little chocolate figurines, tiny bears, marzipan chicks and, of course, eggs of all sizes, ranged along the wonderful old counters of worn-out, chocolate brown wood. The shop is always inventing new delights, but the bulk of its production is based on ancient family recipes. Tasty bites take you back to childhood centuries ago.

The shop today hasn't changed since the end of the 19th century. It attracts everyone from families to sweet enthusiasts to serious historians. Pierre-Jean Bernard, a young grocer from Coulommiers, founded the shop on this spot – then an up-and-coming district of Paris – in 1760. In 1807, his daughter, Marie Adelaide, took over. Three years later, Grimod de La Reynière, the most illustrious food critic of his age, praised her shop and the comely beauty of its owner.

They both became famous overnight, and the shop is now named after her. Subsequent generations sustained the quality of its products and its reputation, widening its stock as world-wide groceries became more available, and as sugar became increasingly inexpensive, they concentrated more and more on sweets. In 1985, the renowned chocolatier, Serge Neveu, took over the business and brought it into the modern age, maintaining its quality without losing touch with its golden age.

Address 35 Rue du Faubourg Montmartre, 75009 Paris, +33 (0)1 47 70 83 69 | Getting there Métro to Le Peletier (Line 7); bus 42, 48 or 85 | Hours Mon–Sat 9.30am–8pm, Sun 10am–7.30pm | Tip At no. 31 you'll find the entry to the arcades Verdeau and Jouffroy, among the most delightful 19th-century arcades in the city, where there are a lot of little shops and restaurants. They're only open during the daytime.

2 ___ Ace Mart
Where Korea and Japan join forces

Entering Ace Mart is like walking into a puzzle, unless you're Korean or Japanese, of course, because this is where these two ancient cuisines meet. It's not just that many of the items on display are only labelled in one or other of these languages; the shelves are so densely packed that they dazzle the senses. It's almost as if the staff have a horror of emptiness, because they are continually restocking as soon as any item leaves the store, appearing with boxes containing more mysteries.

In the fresh-produce section, a few familiar items, like pineapples and bananas, peppers and pimentos rub shoulders with strange fruit and vegetables, like combawa (kaffir lime), daikon (a type of white radish), galangal (a spicy root, a bit like ginger), lemon grass and gobo (the root of the burdock plant, which you grate and use as a seasoning) and fresh tofu.

The packaged vegetables are even more bewildering to Western eyes – myriads of varieties of dried mushrooms and seaweeds. Among the curiosities are katsuo ume, a mix of Japanese prunes and dried skipjack tuna; home-made kimchi, a traditional Korean preparation composed of pimento and fermented vegetables, black garlic, darkened by being cooked for a long time in seawater, which is delicious when served with tomato and mozzarella or roasted leg of lamb; kaffir leaves, which give an incredible lemonish taste to stocks; niboshi, boiled salted and dried sardines or anchovies (to serve with miso soups and a soya paste); and sliced ginseng, which comes in golden boxes reflecting its cost.

Ace stocks a huge variety of ready meals, instant soups, curries, noodles and rice dishes and dozens of desserts, including green tea mochi, made with sticky rice flour, as well as tonics, sodas, beers and sakes. And at 18 Rue Thérèse, Ace Gourmet canteen serves dishes to take away or to eat on the spot.

Address 63 Rue Sainte-Anne, 75002 Paris, +33 (0)1 42 97 56 80 | **Getting there** Métro to Quatre-Septembre (Line 3); bus 21, 27, 39 or 68 | **Hours** Daily 11am–10pm | **Tip** Have a look at Passage Choiseul (one of the few still in its original condition) where the writer Louis-Ferdinand Céline grew up (at nos. 64 and 67), which he describes in his writing.

3 __ Aki Boulanger
French and Japanese baking – real food fusion

Aki Boulanger makes a complete range of classic French breads and a selection of Japanese baking – and several imaginative mixes between the two. Everything is artisanal; the breads are kneaded on the spot and cooked in Aki's own ovens. They've managed, very cleverly, to combine the perfection of French traditional techniques with the subtlety of the Japanese craft. So you will find at Aki, side by side with the familiar baguette, a whole range of original creations such as: garlic, poppy and sesame seed bread; very soft white bread; melon bread (a sweet Japanese brioche); a rose and adzuki (red beans) brioche; green tea viennoiseries; Castella (Portuguese sponge cake reinterpreted in a Japanese way); kinako doughnuts (made with sweet soya flour); a sausage and a curry doughnut; and a yuzu (a kind of citrus) cornet. The pâtisseries tend to be more traditional: strawberry cake; yuzu and strawberry mille-feuille; green tea flan; blueberry cheesecake; rolled matcha cake; and chocolate raspberry cake.

The sandwich and bento selection is so rich I found it difficult to make a choice. The sandwiches include cheese / olive, ham / tomato / olive, tuna / corn, fried pork, eggs, fried pumpkin and the classic ham / cheese. When choosing a bento, it's best to ask for information. They include: onigiri chicken / katsu sauce (stuffed rice balls with a sweet and sour sauce), don fried chicken (in a ginger marinade), mixed salads, and a speciality of the day… As for drinks: coffee, caffè crema, hot chocolate, six different teas, iced tea, coffee and chocolate and, when in season, calpis (a beverage of fermented milk), canned waters, sodas and teas.

The staff is 100 per cent Japanese, and immaculately polite. You can eat on the spot inside or on the terrace outside, or choose a bento to take away. At number 11 bis of the same street, you will find the restaurant Aki, a real Japanese canteen.

Matcha Melon Pain
抹茶メロンパン
2.80€
3.10€ sur place
店内でのお召し上がり

Cacao Melon Pain
カカオメロンパン
2.50€
2.80€ sur place
店内でのお召し上がり

Mochi Goma Anpain
Pâte de riz au sésame et haricot rouge
もち胡麻あんぱん
2.60€
2.80€ sur place
店内でのお召し上がり

Matcha Mochi Anpain
Pâte de riz au thé vert et haricot rouge
抹茶もちあんぱん
2.80€
3.10€ sur place
店内でのお召し上がり

Address 16 Rue Sainte-Anne, 75001 Paris, +33 (0)1 40 15 63 38 | **Getting there** Métro to Pyramides (Line 7 or 14); bus 21, 27, 29, 68, 81 or 95 | **Hours** Mon–Sat 7.30am–8.30pm | **Tip** The building at 12 Rue Sainte-Anne was the site of the night-club La Vie Parisienne, opened by Suzy Solidor, the archetypal *garçonne des années folles* (women dressed as men in the Roaring Twenties) in 1932. One of the first lesbian cabarets in Paris, it enjoyed the patronage of Jean Cocteau, and the young Charles Trenet used to sing there.

Matcha Anpain   Marbré Chocolat

4 Angelina

A sumptuous place to take a sip

Angelina's hot chocolate rapidly acquired a mythic status. It's called 'The African', made from three sorts of cacao beans from Niger, Ghana and Ivory Coast. The blend was created especially for Angelina, and its recipe has remained a closely guarded secret. Angelina's other speciality is its 'Mont-Blanc', an elaborate concoction of meringue, a light Chantilly cream and vermicelli of chestnut cream. Few customers can resist trying one. The tearoom changes its range of pâtisseries twice a year, nuts and chocolates for the winter season, fresh fruits for the summer season – all variations on the classics of French pastries, inspired by the Chef Pâtissier. The delicatessen shop sells teas, confectionery, nut and chocolate spreads, caramels and many more fine treats. And you can also buy their famous chocolate drink in bottles to heat up for a touch of hot luxury at home.

The Austrian confectioner Antoine Rumpelmayer created his tearoom in 1903 and named it after his daughter-in-law, Angelina. The Belle Époque architect, Édouard-Jean Niermans conceived the elegant décor, which remains in place today. Immediately Angelina opened it became a meeting place for the Parisian aristocracy. Marcel Proust, Coco Chanel and the most famous French couturiers became habitués, and the upper echelons of society have flocked there ever since.

Angelina's used to be an exclusive venue on the Rue de Rivoli, but now it's spreading to other refined addresses. There are two Angelinas in Versailles, in the Pavillon d'Orléans and the Petit Trianon, one in the Louvre, in the Richelieu Wing, and, since 2016, they have a summer presence in the Hôtel National des Invalides. Angelina's leather chairs, carpeted floors and chandeliers are the height of aristocratic elegance. The place would be quiet were it not for the crowds. The only drawback is that you almost always have to queue.

Address 226 Rue de Rivoli, 75001 Paris, +33 (0)1 42 60 82 00 | Getting there Métro to Les Tuileries (Line 1); bus 21, 67, 72, 74, 76, 81 or 85 | Hours Mon–Fri 7.30am–7pm, Sat, Sun & holidays 8.30am–7pm | Tip A healthy walk – good for the digestion – in the elegant Jardin des Tuileries, the oldest and the most important French-style garden in the capital, just opposite, is recommended. From here you can reach the Musée de l'Orangerie and the Galerie du Jeu de Paume.

5 L'As du Fallafel

Falafel or shawarma?

Falafel are Middle Eastern, deep-fried, spicy chickpea or broad bean balls. Shawarma are shavings of grilled meat – usually chicken or turkey. Both are served in a pitta bread envelope, with thinly sliced vegetables (cabbage, cucumber, aubergine and tomato) and the whole thing drizzled with a delicious white sesame sauce. Most people eat them while walking in the street. Then the juices run over your fingers making what can only be described as a big mess, which the child in everyone loves.

If you don't mind admitting you're a grown-up, you can sit in the restaurant with the falafel or shawarma served on a plate, with a helping of French fries on the side. You also then have a choice of several Israeli dishes: hummus; aubergine salad; grilled peppers; minced liver, lamb or chicken; merguez (little spicy North African lamb sausages); or chicken pieces fried in batter and breadcrumbs, with a curry sauce. For drinks they serve fresh fruit juices, fizzy drinks and beers and wine from France and Israel.

Serving between 1,500 and 3,000 falafel and shawarma every day, L'As du Fallafel is without doubt the champion of the Rue des Rosiers. This family business, operating since 1979, has become almost a Parisian institution. Photos hang on the walls of the waiters rubbing shoulders with stars like Madonna and Lenny Kravitz. One of the managers assured us that here 'people know what they eat for all the products are fresh and under the control of the Beth Din' (the Jewish Religious Consistory of Paris).

The queue never stops from noon to midnight, but the skilful waiters know how to keep the service moving. If you're desperately hungry, or normally impatient, there are other falafel sellers in the street… though aficionados of L'As du Fallafel swear they're not as good – not that any would dare to admit they'd tried. Try to avoid Sundays when there's no room anywhere.

Address 32–34 Rue des Rosiers, 75004 Paris, +33 (0)1 48 87 63 60 | **Getting there**
Métro to St-Paul (Line 1); bus 29 or 67 | **Hours** Sun–Thu 11am–midnight, Fri 11am
till the hour of Shabbat | **Tip** At no. 10 a small doorway gives access to the Jardin des
Rosiers-Joseph Migneret (who was a famous Resistance fighter) where the remains of
the ancient town wall from the time of Philippe-Auguste (1165–1223) can be seen.

6　Au Bout du Champs

Picked in the morning for you in the evening

In 2014, Joseph Petit paced across the fields around Paris looking for local produce that he could sell directly to customers. Julien Adam soon joined him and together they opened their chain of vegetable and fruit shops, which now number seven. The idea is simple, but perfect. The produce in their shops is entirely seasonal and local; they make no effort to supplement their shelves with distantly-grown fruit and vegetables brought in from a market. What's more, almost all their produce is harvested that morning for sale in the afternoon, which explains their late opening hours. You can't get food fresher or more local than this.

All the farmers they work with follow organic principles and they stock the mushrooms and endives of the only urban organic farm of Paris, La Caverne. In front of every crate of vegetables and fruit they give the name and location of every farmer, and, on bits of cardboard, list recipes, such as cooking aubergine with a miso (soya bean) paste, making a green soup with cucumber or a beetroot or courgette salad. They give useful tips too – such as how to keep your herbs fresh by wrapping them in a damp tea towel. But they take care to warn you – this is not the usual supermarket fare: you have to wash their potatoes thoroughly, and the leeks, turnips and beetroot have a lot of flaws – but, my goodness, do they taste good!

Au Bout du Champs also sell new-laid eggs (they ask you to bring back the boxes so that there's no waste), and they recommend that you don't keep them in the fridge because this makes the shells fragile.

They also stock locally made honeys, jams, linseed, poppy and rape oils, and an excellent apple juice sold in a five-litre box. They offer families who have pets at home succulent cuttings from their vegetables and fruit. And after closing time on Sundays they put what they haven't sold on the pavement for anyone to take.

Address 28 Rue Daguerre, 75014 Paris | **Getting there** Métro to Denfert-Rochereau (Line 4 or 6); bus 38 or 68 | **Hours** Mon, Tue, Thu, Fri 4–8pm, Wed, Sat, Sun 10am–8pm | **Tip** At 5 Rue Schoelcher you will find the Institut Giacometti, where there is a reconstruction of the artist's studio that evokes his idiosyncratic working environment. The Institute is housed in a beautiful Art Deco mansion, once the studio of the artist and interior designer Paul Follot. Visits bookable in advance only (see www.fondation-giacometti.fr).

7__Autour du Saumon

Salmon in its prime glory

Salmon has suffered a sorry history in recent years, with stocks almost disappearing in the wild while at the same time it's been cruelly and debilitatingly farmed.

This shop treats this noble fish with all the respect it deserves. The strictest selection of products guarantees quality, freshness and traceability. In the beautiful, specially refrigerated window display, are rows of salmon fillets, with colours ranging from gold to a sunset glow. They come from Norway, Shetland, the Faroes and France, with organic salmon from Ireland and Scotland and wild salmon from the Baltic, all immaculately hand-sliced.

The shop also stocks a high-quality range of other products: dried fish roes, salmon eggs; Kaviari caviar, squid ink and tarama; bonito; sardines; Ortiz tuna belly; cod liver; smoked herring; salmon, mackerel and scallop rillettes plus several caviars, one of them an Osciètre and a Baeri farm-bred one from Aquitaine. At the deli counter, ready-made dishes include: plain, crab or wasabi tarama; truffle risotto; prawns in parsley, Scandinavian style or Kashmiri (made with coconut milk); marinated herrings and blinis. They also stock a fine selection of wines and vodkas, jams, orange marmalade, Spanish cold meats, olive oil and high-quality preserves including fig, onion and tomato chutneys, ketchup, Kalamata olive cream, Kalamata figs and foie gras.

You can walk through to the little restaurant next door, with its sober Scandinavian décor. They serve lunch with a set menu, two different salmons, a glass of wine and coffee with petits fours. And for dinner, their excellent menu is based on salmon and other fish, with starters, salads, hot or cold dishes, all large, generously garnished servings, and desserts. You can also choose a Menu des Gourmets with four different dishes and caviar. Autour du Saumon has several outlets in Paris and maintains its high standards everywhere.

Address 60 Rue François Miron, 75004 Paris, +33 (0)1 42 77 23 08 | **Getting there** Métro to Saint-Paul (Line 1); bus 67, 69, 76 or 96 | **Hours** Mon–Sat 9.30am–10pm, Sun 10am–8pm | **Tip** The Saint-Paul-Saint-Louis church in Rue Saint-Antoine is a 17th-century Baroque church where you can see Eugène Delacroix's dramatic painting *Christ in Agony on the Mount of Olives*. There are also two stoups (holy water vessels) in the form of shells presented to the church by Victor Hugo on the occasion of the marriage of his daughter.

8 Aux Merveilleux de Fred
Mountain peaks of meringues

The merveilleux is a traditional pâtisserie of northern France and Flanders. It consists of two meringues sandwiched together with Chantilly cream, then rolled in chocolate flakes and crumbled 'speculoos' (gingersnaps). For a long time this traditional, rather heavy cake was neglected, until 1985, when Frédéric Vaucamps, in his pâtisserie in Lille, adapted the old recipe to modern tastes, making it much lighter and adding a spectrum of other flavours. The name *merveilleux* means 'marvellous', but it was also a name given to one of the eccentric fashions that blossomed after the Revolution. Vaucamps had the bright idea of naming his new cakes after other fashions.

The Incroyable (incredible) is garnished with speculoos whipped cream and encrusted with white chocolate flakes. The Impensable (unthinkable) is made with coffee cream sandwiched between two crystalised coffee meringues. The Merveilleux itself is now garnished with chocolate cream and a coating of black chocolate flakes. The Magnifique is filled with praline cream and has a covering of caramelised hazelnuts and almond flakes. The Sans-Culotte (named after the heroic lower classes of the Revolution) is made with caramel cream and a coating of crystallised meringue. The Excentrique is filled with cherry cream. All of them are as light as air and melt when your tongue lifts them to the roof of your mouth. They come in mini and individual portions, and as much bigger cakes, varying in size from 4 to 24 helpings. As a tempting starter, the pâtisserie offers an assortment of minis in ravishing boxes.

The pâtisserie now has seven addresses in Paris as well as shops in Lille, Bordeaux, Nantes, Brussels, Berlin, Geneva, London and New York. In each shop the cakes are made in front of the clients. Everything is designed to tempt you to taste – even if you don't have a sweet tooth. Those who do are doomed.

Address 24 Rue du Pont Louis-Philippe, 75004 Paris, +33 (0)1 57 40 98 43 | **Getting there** Métro to Saint-Paul (Line 1); bus 69, 76 or 96 | **Hours** Tue–Sat 9am–8pm, Sun 9am–7pm | **Tip** In the same street you can find two special paper shops, Papier Plus and Caligrane, both of which offer exceptional papers of remarkable quality.

9_ Beillevaire
The fascination of a profession

Pascal Beillevaire started his business in the most modest way, by selling milk and cream from his family's farm at local markets. He became fascinated, however, with dairy products, and during his holidays he travelled all over France with his wife Claudine, researching the best cheeses of every terroir, in order to introduce them to his clients. One step led to another, and he started to make, refine and age excellent cheeses of his own.

His produce is now made with raw milk, which has been collected from milk producers less than 10 kilometres from his Fromagerie at Machecoul in the Vendée. The products include raw butter, raw cream, natural and fruit yoghurts, rice pudding, crème brûlée, semolina pudding, chocolate vanilla or pistachio cream, and local cheeses like Machecoul, Mojette, Pont d'Yeu (a goat's cheese) or Rocher Nantais. His cheese shops now age cheeses from all over France, with some from abroad: Beaufort de Savoie, Bleu d'Auvergne, Bûche de chèvre from the Marais Poitevin; Grise des Volcans from the Auvergne; Morbier from the Jura; tomme from Corsica; Mimolette and Vacherin from the Mont d'Or; Munster Fermier; and Gruyère from the high summer meadows of Switzerland.

The Beillevaire shops offer sandwiches, the recipes for which change every week and are made in their shop in the 15th Arrondissement. I tried a Brillat-Savarin with figs and nuts; the Rocher Nantais, smoked turkey with sun-dried tomatoes; the Long Cendré, with chicken, ras-el-hanout and tapenade. Perfect.

Beillevaire also offers cheese plates to order, jams, olive oil and a delicious gingerbread (a spicebread without ginger). Recipes can be provided and visits to the Fromagerie in Machecoulais, with simple tastings or a whole cheese meal. My favourite shop is the one on the Rue Delambre, where the staff are exceptionally knowledgeable, but all 13 Beillevaire shops are excellent.

Address 8 Rue Delambre, 75014 Paris, +33 (0)1 42 79 00 40 | **Getting there** Métro to Vavin (Line 4); bus 58, 68, 82 or 91 | **Hours** Tue–Fri 8.30am–1pm & 4–8pm, Sat 8.30am–1.30pm & 3.30–8pm, Sun 9am–1pm | **Tip** At 26 Rue Vavin, there is a fine white-tiled building designed by Henri Sauvage in 1912 in a style somewhere between Art Nouveau and Art Moderne. The architect designed several other notable buildings in Paris.

10_Les Belles Envies
Sugar-free pâtisseries!

Alixe Boron, a frustrated diabetic, opened this pâtisserie to please all fellow sufferers who want to eat sweets without taking risks. They don't use white flour, only lupin flour and half wholemeal flour. All beet and cane sugar is replaced by sugar extracted from coconut. But beware: this is still sugar, even if the glycaemic index is controlled.

All the ingredients and finished products are validated by a diabetologist: the sesame, sea salt, grilled almonds, the dark and the white chocolate bars, the macadamia and grilled hazelnut milk bars, the marbled loaf, the lemon loaf, the chocolate sticks and the cookies. Astonishingly, they even make a gluten-free chocolate spread with milk and hazelnuts but no sugar. The individual chocolates flavoured with fruit, pepper, coconut or peanut, are absolutely delicious.

To begin, I recommend the Coffret Dégustation of 18 pieces, at a very reasonable price. The pâtisseries, such as the Suprême Cacahuète (with peanut), the Tartelette Fruits Rouges (with red berries), the Œuf Choco Passion (with chocolate and passion fruit), the Yuzu Mandarine (with tangerine) and the Carrément Chocolat are all mouth-wateringly good. And these flavours change according to the seasons. No strawberries and cherries at Christmas!

Everything is made on the spot in the immaculate kitchen just behind the shop. A large window lets you see what's going on (mind you, the door is often left open too). There's a busy yet friendly atmosphere about the whole place. You can make yourself at home in the little tearoom or on a tiny terrace on the pavement outside. The staff are genuinely involved and happy to explain the products and the processes to you. It's certainly caught the wave of its time, but it's a beautiful and sincere initiative, and what they produce is excellent. You can buy online, and they deliver throughout Paris.

Address 3 Rue Monge, 75005 Paris, +33 (0)1 42 38 01 41. Also at 17 Rue Poncelet, 75017 Paris | **Getting there** Métro to Maubert-Mutualité (Line 10); bus 47, 86 or 87 | **Hours** Tue–Sat 10am–8pm, Sun 10am–7pm | **Tip** At 6 Place Paul-Painlevé you can find the Musée de Cluny with its great medieval collection, where you can see the breathtaking tapestry *The Lady and the Unicorn*.

11 __ Berthillon

The most famous Parisian ice cream maker

The reputation of the Maison Berthillon is beyond question but the ice creams are of such quality that it seems difficult to ignore them. Every day, 1,000 litres of ice creams and sorbets made on the Île Saint-Louis will delight the customers in the shop but also in 140 restaurants, brasseries, chocolatiers and delicatessens in the Paris region, and the rest of France.

The ice creams are made with milk, crème fraîche, sugar, fresh eggs and natural flavours (vanilla pods, cocoa butter); the sorbets are pure fruit and sugar. The production, which remains artisanal, depends on what's good in the market, and only the best is selected. More than 70 flavours await you. Alongside the traditional flavours are caramel and nougatine, chocolate with nougat, foie gras, almond milk, lavender, gingerbread, lemon praliné and coriander, Earl Grey tea and tiramisu. Among the sorbets, roasted pineapple and fresh basil, raspberry and rose, wild strawberries, lychee, wild peach, daiquiri and lemon thyme. Some of the blends are particularly delicious and a real success, like hazelnut and wild strawberries, pear and caramel, apricot and raspberry.

There are specialities for eight people, like tarte Tatin ice cream (vanilla, caramel, apple), the pina colada (rum, raisins, coconut and pineapple), the Belle Hélène (vanilla, pear, caramelised pears, to serve with a cocoa or raspberry coulis), as well as the bombes glacées like the Bombe Alexandra (round dome) wild peach sorbet filled with fine champagne, a type of Cognac, or the Bombe Opéra (chocolate ice cream filled with coffee parfait) an ice cream, warm-fluffed above a bowl of hot water. All are absolutely remarkable.

In collaboration with the Poilâne bakery, Berthillon has created a Punitions (punishment) shortbread ice cream and a Mirabelle sorbet with Poilâne granola. The tearoom next door is a real little jewel and offers pâtisseries.

Address 29–31 Rue Saint-Louis en l'Île, 75004 Paris, +33 (0)1 43 54 31 61 | Getting there Métro to Pont Marie (Line 7); bus 24, 63, 67, 86 or 87 | Hours Wed–Sun 10am–8pm | Tip At 19, l'Église Saint-Louis-en-l'Île, an elaborate Baroque church built between 1624 and 1726, is definitely worth a visit. But take a stroll around the island too. Together with the Île de la Cité, it is one of two natural islands in the Seine.

12 Bidoche
Meat for the enthusiast

My research for this book led me, by chance, to Bidoche just as the semi-final of the World Cup 2018 was being played. There was no one in the shop; everyone was in the restaurant behind watching the match. Alexander de Toulmon immediately came out and answered all my questions enthusiastically, despite the pull of the roars from the room behind. I knew I was dealing with a real aficionado. Originally working as a banker, for a time in New York, he decided to return to his main love. *La Bidoche* is a French slang word for 'meat'. He did his apprenticeship with, among others, Hugo Desnoyer, and opened his butchery in 2017. It immediately earned the approval of his peers, and began to attract customers far and wide.

Alexander specialises in pure French breeds, taking care about rearing and killing methods. He hangs his meat for at least 30 days, and uses the traditional cuts long proven to bring out the best flavour in the meat. For beef and veal, he favours the Limousine (from the Limoges area) and the Bazadaise (a breed from south of the Gironde Estuary). For lamb, he chooses Baronet du Limousin and Pré salé of Mont Saint-Michel, sheep that graze on the salt marshes that are covered by the high tide. For pork, it's Pays Basque and Auvergne. The poultry come from the Landes (an area between Bordeaux and Spain famed for its fowls).

Behind the butchery is a restaurant. There's a charcuterie dish, a seasonal salad and a beef, veal or lamb tartare (raw). The main dishes are L'Assiette de Bidoche (three grilled hunks of beef, mutton and pork) or the same trio as a tartare. The restaurant also serves a vegetarian steak made with bulgur wheat, green lentils and breadcrumbs, for partners with reservations about eating meat. For the real enthusiasts, you can choose a cut of meat in the butchery and have it cooked with the accompaniment you fancy. Meat at its best.

Address 7 Rue du Jean-Pierre Timbaud, 75011 Paris, +33 (0)9 81 12 59 81 | **Getting there** Métro to Filles du Calvaire (Line 8) or to Oberkampf (Line 5 or 9); bus 56 or 96 | **Hours** Tue–Sat 9.30am–1pm & 4.30–10.30pm, Sun 9.30am–1pm | **Tip** At 110 Rue Amelot you will find the Cirque d'Hiver Bouglione, built in 1852, a classified historic monument and one of the oldest constructed circuses in Europe. And just next to it, on Rue Amelot, is the excellent and beautiful restaurant, the Clown Bar.

13＿BMK

The best of African flavours in a little place

BMK is an explosion of magic on an offbeat street. Fousseyni Djikine, originally from Mali, quit his job as a consultant to open what has become the trendiest African canteen in Paris. These days there is almost always a crowd at the door, eager to get in.

A blackboard in the window highlights the special spirit of this place. The day I went I was invited to discover the Moringa, the tree of a thousand virtues, known in English as the Horseradish Tree. It's a plant that contains 7 times the quantity of vitamin C found in oranges, 4 times the calcium in milk and 25 times the iron in spinach! You can't help but be drawn inside. The shelves groan with exotic products: purée of extra-strong pimento and ginger, flour and couscous of cassava, crème niébé (a type of bean), cream of pimento, crème safou (a type of wild plum), Joe & Avrel's cream of ginger, cassava leaves, chips made from fried plantain, biltong (marinated with dried chilli), oil of macadamia nut and sesame, baobab and guava jam, artisanal chocolate from the Ivory Coast, tisane d'amour, teas and African coffees, organic rooibos tea (green or peach-flavoured), and panamako (hibiscus juice from Burkina Faso with Touraine apple).

Everything is made in-house, and all the meat is French. There are nine African dishes: mafés (beef-based), yassas (chicken-based) and thiebs (fish-based) each with a vegetarian or vegan alternative; three African-inspired salads, two without gluten, served with a mix of French fries made from cassava, yam and sweet potato, with a sesame mayonnaise. For dessert, chocolate cake, banana bread and a fresh fruit salad. Every day there's a different starter, main dish, dessert and a sandwich, all announced on a slate near the magnificent portrait of Nelson Mandela. To drink, there's fruit juice, infusions, teas and coffee. The welcome is so warm it's tropical. You almost feel like you are in Africa!

Address 14 Rue de la Fidélité, 75010 Paris, +33 (0)9 82 54 17 48 | Getting there
Métro to Gare de l'Est or Château d'Eau (Line 4, 5 or 7); bus 31, 38, 39 or 65 | Hours
Tue – Sat noon – 10.30pm | Tip At 28 Boulevard de Bonne Nouvelle you can visit the
Musée Gourmand du Chocolat, which tells the story of the origin, production and
consumption of chocolate, with educational activities and workshops for children.

14__Bogato
Cakes with lashings of fun

Bogato's most famous dish is their sweet burger – it's been copied by hundreds of pâtisseries. It looks like the real thing but it's made with macaron, chocolate, raspberries and fresh mint. You can taste one in the shop, while sipping tea, coffee, fruit juice or fizzy drinks when seated at the vintage '50s tables. Or, if you prefer, you can try one of their other hot sellers: a Chalala – a girlie pink strawberry cake but with a surprise rose flavour, with a pretty little bow on top.

Everything in Bogato springs from the imagination of Anaïs Olmer, the shop's creator and owner. She was trained at the famous Penninghen Art School, and then went into advertising. But she soon became fed up with the time it took for projects to reach fruition. She wanted immediate results and direct contact with her clients. She trained as a pâtissière and soon realised that there was a gap in the market. There were no fun cakes custom-made for children, except for commonplace sweets sold in bakers and supermarkets. Thinking of children, she released the inventiveness in herself.

In 2010, Anaïs opened Bogato with a young Japanese pâtissière. The business took off and now has a team of 13. Anaïs wanted bright colours, festive fun with a good helping of insolent cheek. She writes the recipes and designs the cakes, often tailor-made for special occasions, according to the interests of the clients. You can order a cake shaped like a medieval castle, a dinosaur or a Wonder Woman bra.

Bogato now provides everything you need for a party to go with a swing, including interior design, animation and music. The shop also sells many special gadgets connected with pâtisserie – moulds and colouring, candles and decorations. They also run cookery workshops where children can make real cakes to specific recipes but decorate them themselves. Invention is like spilling beans at Bogato.

Address 7 Rue Liancourt, 75014 Paris, +33 (0)1 40 47 03 51 | **Getting there** Métro to Denfert-Rochereau (Line 4); bus 38 or 68 | **Hours** Tue–Sat 10am–7pm | **Tip** On the Place Denfert-Rochereau you can visit the dramatic Catacombes de Paris, a municipal ossuary that dates back to the 17th century, situated in ancient quarries. But you'll need to go early, as the queue to get in can be almost as long as the catacombs themselves!

15 Bouillon Chartier

Good food for the people

The Bouillon Chartier is just as it was when it first opened in 1896. The two brothers, Frédéric and Camille Chartier had a simple idea: to offer full, sustaining meals at a very reasonable price. Their aim was to attract loyal clients, and the hundreds of wooden drawers containing the napkins of their regulars prove their success in this. Chartier's huge salon in its original Belle Époque style is still situated at the end of an unassuming cul-de-sac. It's now a classified Historic Monument. But this status hasn't given it airs and graces. Fifty million meals after it first opened, it remains one of the cheapest basic restaurants in Paris.

On the menu, are the classic dishes of France – which are becoming rarer as they're replaced by trendier, international cuisine. Among the starters are egg mayonnaise, celeriac remoulade, snails, beef muzzle with vinaigrette – all about €5. For the main course there's chicken with French fries, garnished sauerkraut, andouillette with mustard sauce, rump steak and spaghetti bolognaise – all for around €10. Desserts include rum baba with Chantilly cream, chocolate mousse, puff pastry choux with ice cream and hot chocolate, or Mont Blanc – all for about €4. The wine of the month is no more than €13.

No wonder there are always queues to get in. But with 320 places, the queue moves pretty quickly. And once you're in you don't have to wait long. The waiters are superb professionals, working with extreme rapidity between the tables. They all wear the traditional French waiter's outfit, the 'rondin' (a black waistcoat with a long white apron). They eschew modern computers, using instead their phenomenal memories. But they do note your orders on the paper tablecloths as you make them, so they can tot your bill up easily at the end. The din of happy clients is, however, tremendous; it's not a place to take a first date.

Address 7 Rue du Faubourg Montmartre, 75009 Paris, +33 (0)1 47 70 86 29 | **Getting there** Métro to Rue Montmartre (Line 8 or 9); bus 20, 39, 48, 67, 74 or 85 | **Hours** Daily 11.30am – midnight, no reservations | **Tip** At 10 Boulevard Montmartre is the Musée Grévin, one of the oldest waxwork museums in Europe, founded in 1882. Here you can see reproductions of famous people in wax, a big showroom, and a Palais des Mirages, based on optical illusions.

16__Bouillon Pigalle
The ultimate soup kitchen, French-style

Bouillon in French means 'stock' – the essential ingredient of soup. Bouillon-style restaurants were the French equivalent of English soup kitchens, which during the last century used to make good food available at reasonable prices for the working classes. Bouillon Pigalle is a superb modern version of this traditional type of catering, created by the Moussie brothers and opened in 2017.

The atmosphere is at once rich, colourful and accessible, both modern and traditional. The vast ground floor is light and airy, lit by large windows, with long tables set with red plastic imitation-leather benches and bentwood chairs, against walls decorated with mirrors and faïence tiles, and the waiters all wear black waistcoats. This is where the Belle Époque meets the 21st century. Upstairs, the effect is more plush, with dark red velvet boudoir seats on a terrace overlooking the Place Pigalle.

This 300-seater restaurant serves about 1,000 meals a day, but with a quality control that is seriously impressive. The menu is the brainchild of the chef, Clement Chicard. Every dish is a French classic and 100 per cent home-made. In all there are only 15 starters, 14 main courses and 10 desserts. Starters include celeriac remoulade, snails in parsley butter and smoked sprats specially supplied by the famous fishmonger, Petrossian. Main courses include veal head with the traditional gribiche sauce generously garnished with fresh herbs, and delicious French equivalents of the familiar English working-class dishes, cauliflower cheese and bangers and mash. Puddings include chocolate profiteroles, Paris-Brest made tangy with a little salt and a delicious rum baba with Chantilly cream. The drinks, whether wine, beer or coke, are served in standard Bouillon Pigalle carafes, in three sizes – small, magnum and jeroboam. But amazingly the price of a meal averages out at about €15 per person.

Address 22 Boulevard de Clichy, 75018 Paris, +33 (0)1 42 59 69 31 | **Getting there** Métro to Pigalle (Line 2 or 12); bus 30, 54 or 67 | **Hours** Daily noon – midnight, no reservations | **Tip** At 16 Rue Chaptal, in a house dating from 1830, there's the Musée de la Vie Romantique, which has one floor dedicated to the writer George Sand.

17__Boulangerie Liberté

A warm feeling outside and in

I discovered Liberté when walking along the Rue de Ménilmontant and was immediately attracted to its long façade of tall windows, behind which was an open bakery where people were working adjacent to a café area packed with long tables where customers were enjoying themselves eating and talking. The warmth and friendliness of the place drew me in from the street. Benoît Castel created Liberté with the idea of demystifying baking and pâtisserie making, to show how everything works, creating a relaxed, confident relationship between his (very friendly) staff and his (very eager) customers. And you can see it working from across the street!

Star among the breads on offer is the Liberté Loaf – made with liquid yeast and very carefully selected flours (as is true of all their products). They also make a Pain du Coin (a play on words in French meaning both 'corner' and 'quince'), made with rye flour, honey, quince and smoked salt. They offer a traditional baguette made with natural yeast and Camargue salt, a Granola Bread made with walnuts, hazelnuts, raisins and seeds, a Pain Complet and a Baltic Loaf made with a dozen different cereals.

Their viennoiseries range from croissants to pain aux raisins and pain au chocolat and apple turnovers. The pâtisseries are made without any unnecessary frills, and are perfect. Try Castel's emblematic cheesecake, plain or raspberry, or the cherry clafoutis. The moelleux au chocolat – a cake with crusty outside and soft inside – is superb. They also make a lemon tart, and a mille-feuille with chocolate or vanilla, and you only have to look at one of his beautiful madeleines to want to eat it.

Saturday and Sunday is brunch time – an open buffet with mixed salads, charcuterie boards, roast chicken, caramelised pork, seasonal vegetables, viennoiseries, fruit and dessert. Once you know about this place, it's hard to stay outside.

Address 150 Rue de Ménilmontant, 75020 Paris, +33 (0)1 46 36 13 82 | **Getting there** Métro to Pelleport (Line 3bis); bus 60, 61 or 96 | **Hours** Wed–Fri 7.30am–8pm, Sat 8am–8pm, Sun 8am–6pm | **Tip** At no. 121, the Pavillon Carré de Baudouin, previously a neoclassical folly with a Palladian façade, dating back to 1770, has been restored and is now a lively cultural centre.

18 Boulevard Raspail Organic Food Market

The biggest and best organic market in Paris

The traditional market of the Boulevard Raspail was extended in 1989 into an organic market, held only on Sundays. Everyone in the neighbourhood goes. Here you are very likely to bump into famous figures from the media and politics. It's held in the leafy central alley of the boulevard, which makes you feel you're in the country, far from the noise and traffic of the city.

There are about 50 stalls, all certified for the quality and credentials of their products. There's a huge choice of fresh vegetables, fruit, herbs, and aromatic plants like mustard, nasturtium and lavender. There are stalls selling fish and seafood and others stacked high with cheeses, creams and yoghurts, while others specialise in meat, poultry and eggs or in wines and fruit juices, or honeys, jams and spreads. Then there's an array of bakers, with a range of breads, some made of spelt, others gluten-free, and fine displays of viennoiseries and pâtisseries, cakes, biscuits and shortbreads, savoury and sweet tarts and quiches.

There are tempting aromas everywhere. Several stalls offer dishes to take away: meals with quinoa, buckwheat, grilled pumpkin, wok-tossed vegetables, red rice tagliatelles with vegetables and ginger, quinoa stuffed courgettes, paella with seaweeds, green Lebanese taboulé, chick peas with salt cod…

Most tempting of all are the delights to nibble on the spot: vegetable and tofu turnovers, vegetable and tuna or potato bricks, pizzas, gougères (cheese pastries – a particular favourite of mine) and galettes (little pancakes). A visit to this market usually turns into a picnic, not just a shopping trip. There are a few stalls selling organic beauty products and health-giving drinks, and scattered in between are stands displaying handmade crafts like the beautiful turned bowls of the carpenter Desmond Corcoran.

Address Along the Boulevard Raspail, between Rue du Cherche Midi and Rue de Rennes, 75006 Paris | **Getting there** Métro to Rennes (Line 12) or Saint-Placide (Line 4); bus 58, 68 or 89 | **Hours** Sun 9am – 3pm | **Tip** At Boulevard Raspail you can see a 19th-century neo-Gothic house with a bestiary of fantastic animals on the top-floor balcony.

19__Bustronome
Slow food on the move

There's a new buzz word in France – bistronomie. It's a fusion between 'bistro food' and 'gastronomy'. No one knows the origin of the word 'bistro'. Some think it derives from the Russian word meaning 'hurry', shouted at waiters by Russians who opened restaurants in Paris after 1917. Whatever, 'bistro' means 'quick food'. But Bustronome serves bistronomie, slow food, on the go. It's a brilliant idea – you eat in style in a slow-moving restaurant, enjoying the ever-changing scenery of Paris.

The luxury double-decker restaurant bus starts at the foot of the Arc de Triomphe, on the corner of Avenue Kleber. The upper deck has been converted into an elegant restaurant, comfortably seating 38 guests. The open kitchen is downstairs. Much of the food is initially prepared in a central kitchen but a chef is always on board to cook the last stages and give the finishing touches to the dishes. For lunch we had tomato gazpacho with fresh goat's cheese followed by lightly cooked bream, with a cream of green peas and polenta with vanilla butter. Also on offer was Marengo veal fillet with garlic and white wine (a dish beloved by Napoleon), followed by a rum baba with amaretto or apricot compote with thyme and whipped cream. The evening meal is a bit more sophisticated with an extra course, offering langoustine with lime zest, grilled hazelnuts and custard apple or buttered pigeon fillet in a cauliflower crust with tiny new potatoes, watercress and red currant jus. The wine list is excellent and matches the food.

The journey goes past many of the finest monuments of Paris – the Opéra Garnier, the Louvre, Notre-Dame, the Eiffel Tower and the Champs de Mars. The bus can be hired for private parties and joined where you are, within reason, and the delightful, friendly staff enhance one's enjoyment of this slow culinary drift through the capital of food.

Address Place Charles de Gaulle Étoile, corner of Avenue Kléber, 75016 Paris, +33 (0)9 54 44 45 55 | **Getting there** Métro to Charles de Gaulle-Étoile (Line 6); bus 22, 30, 31 or 52 | **Hours** Daily 12.15pm & 7.45pm (additional dinner Sat & Sun 8.45pm) | **Tip** Reserve your ticket to go to the top of the Arc de Triomphe and enjoy the stupendous views before joining the bus.

20 La Caféothèque

From Guatemala to the banks of the Seine

Gloria Montenegro, once the Guatemalan ambassador to Paris, wanted to change things. In 2001, she left diplomacy to discover what was really going on in the world of coffee, a vital element of her country's economy. Her research led her to found the *caféologie*, a listing of 'the taste, smell, and appearance of coffees coming from different terroirs,' and an academy to analyse coffee samples and offer teaching programmes for professionals. A great number of the best Parisian baristas (coffee specialists) have gone through her apprenticeship.

In September 2015, she founded Caféothèque (first called Soluna Cafés). The place is absolutely charming, on the leafy north bank of the Seine. Its relaxed atmosphere is due partly to the fact that it is the café of a busy working institution, which, unusually, is open and welcoming to everyone. Several rooms are amusingly decorated with South American jungle scenery and there's a delightful terrace outside.

Staff select three 'coffees of the day', from different 'terroirs', with all the stages of their preparation, from field to table, openly traceable. The beans are roasted in-house by professionals. The café serves breakfast from 8.30am to midday with orange juice, the coffee of the day with viennoiserie or bread, butter and jam. For lunch they offer, as a set menu, quiche with salad, a dessert and coffee. Other dishes include home-made beef, chicken or vegetarian empanadas with chimichurri and a salad. For dessert: ice creams and sorbets from the Compagnie des Desserts, fruit baba without alcohol or an Opéra (a special chocolate cake) by Gaston Lenôtre. They offer fresh fruit juice cocktails, teas, infusions, hot chocolates, lemonades, milkshakes, beer from the Secret des Moines brewery, wine by the glass or the bottle… and of course a huge range of coffees. They sell them as beans or ground, in the shop.

Address 50–52 Rue de l'Hôtel de Ville, 75004 Paris, +33 (0)1 53 01 83 84 | **Getting there** Métro to Pont-Marie (Line 7); bus 7 or 67 | **Hours** Mon–Fri 8.30am–7.30pm, Sat & Sun 10am–7.30pm | **Tip** Round the corner, at 17 Rue Geoffroy L'Asnier, you can visit the moving Shoah Memorial, Paris' Holocaust museum.

21__Caffè Stern

The height of visual and culinary sophistication

What happens when Massimiliano Alajmo, the Italian prodigy chef (who earned three Michelin stars when he was only 28), his brother Raffaele, the brilliant restaurateur, Gianni Frasi, Italy's supreme *torréfacteur* (coffee-roaster), the star entrepreneur David Lanher and his old friend Philippe Starck, one of the world's most imaginative modern designers, decide to create something together? The result: Caffè Stern – a cavern of magic.

Stern used to be a handsome print-maker's and engraver's shop, dating from 1834 when it was patronised by the Élysée Palace and the elite of French society. The interior décor – much of which remains in situ – is a classified historic monument. Its transformation into an Italian café / bistro / restaurant is a triumph of sensitive imagination. But it provides not only delights for the eye but also for the palate. The cooking expresses the quintessence of Italian cuisine. As Alajmo says, it's 'intense and light, nostalgic and contemporary.'

Here are a few examples of what was on the menu when I visited in February (for everything is seasonal, of course): fried langoustine involtini (delicious bites in little wrapped bundles), battered artichokes and dried fish roe sauce; ravioli stuffed with smoked burrata cheese; roast pigeon with rhubarb, creamed squash and winter vegetables; black rice steamed pizza with black truffle; snail risotto with a smoked beetroot sauce; veal cheek alla canèvera, turmeric purée and bitter chicory; entrecôte steak with seaweed mayonnaise and roasted beetroot. For desserts: grapefruit and mountain pine nut sorbet with lemon confit; panettone of the Sérénissime and spiced tiramisu cream.

During the day, you can stroll in and have a drink – all the wines are Italian – or you can sip a Grappa, cup of tea or coffee with homemade pâtisseries. On the shelves, a number of Italian products are for sale.

Address 47 Passage des Panoramas, 75002 Paris, +33 (0)1 75 43 63 10 | Getting there Métro to Montmartre or Richelieu Drouot (Line 8); bus 20, 39, 48, 67 or 74 | Hours Tue–Sat 9.30am–10.30pm | Tip At 146 Rue Montmartre (corner of Rue du Croissant), you can visit the Café du Croissant where Jean Jaurès, the famous French militant socialist and pacifist, was assassinated by a nationalist student just after the outbreak of war in 1914.

22 Carré Pain de Mie

An international bread exchange

Pain de Mie means the soft middle part of the bread, inside the crust. It looks very like the sliced white loaves you get everywhere in British supermarkets (all artificially manufactured), but it tastes nothing like them, for though Pain de Mie is always white, it's made with the finest quality flour. Pain de Mie is a specialist taste in France, but it is found everywhere in Japan.

Michio Hasegawa had the bright idea to make French Pain de Mie in his bakery in Tokyo. Its huge success led him to return the favour and the flavour to Paris. He founded Carré Pain de Mie, offering loaves made with French flour, which are domed on top, and loaves made with Japanese flour from Hokkaido, which are square. Japanese Pain de Mie comes in three basic types: motchi motchi with an elastic texture like sticky rice; shittori, which is soft and silky; and sakkuri, which is crunchy.

Carré Pain de Mie offers a menu of sandwiches to take away or eat in the light, airy 40-seat café. A team of serious Japanese cooks, in an open kitchen, make your order on the spot. You can taste Tonkatsu, a breadcrumbed pork cutlet served with minced cabbage, a Reuben, with sauerkraut, pastrami and Comté cheese, a Jambon Prince de Paris with ham, egg and lettuce, a Club Carré with toasted bread, free-range chicken, bacon, lettuce, tomato, egg and herb mayonnaise, and a delicious amazing croque-monsieur and croque-madame made with Prince de Paris ham, 15-month-aged Comté and béchamel sauce. The French fries are cooked to order and the sandwiches are served without crusts (though the cut raw crusts are served nicely on the side in a cone and some customers eat them). As a dessert, they offer a sandwich with seasonal fruit and a traditional French dish made with leftover bread fried in butter with sugar and fruit. A slight caveat: the prices are a little high, but well worth it for the superb quality.

Address 5 Rue Rambuteau, 75004 Paris, +33 (0)1 44 54 92 73 | **Getting there** Métro to
Étienne Marcel or Rambuteau (Line 4 or 11); bus 29 | **Hours** Tue–Sun 10am–7pm |
Tip Next to the Centre Pompidou is the Stravinsky fountain by Jean Tinguely and
Niki de Saint Phalle, a masterpiece of playful humour.

23 _ Causses

Food for the stomach and the mind

At Causses, transparency and traceability are the key. This handsome shop is full of wonderful produce, but also full of words. Hanging from the ceiling are posters telling you everything you need to know about the produce on sale below (where it's from, how it's grown, the methods used in its preparation). But first of all you are faced with the agreement signed by all Causses' suppliers that they will abide by the standards set by the shop, inspired by the Slow Food Movement. Causses is nothing if not serious, but in this case serious is not boring, because what's on offer is delicious.

There are, of course, racks of seasonal vegetables, fruit and cheeses (including the superb Comté of Marcel Petite). At the charcuterie there's Bayonne and San Daniele ham, the famous Prince de Paris ham, and many dishes to take away (including roll-mops and octopus salad), and meat (including beef, pork, chicken and duck).

Causses specialises in selling a huge amount of produce *en vrac* (in containers where you help yourself, to avoid unnecessary packaging). There are bins full of olives, dried vegetables, pulses and seeds and olive oil in tanks. There are prepared soups from the Ferme Polder Saint-Michel (including courgettes, tarragon, carrots, red lentils and curry), tinned food and dried products, from sardine rillettes to coq au vin. The wines are carefully chosen as well as the ciders, beers, lemonades and fruit juices. The bread comes from the Dupain bakery and from Benoît Castel. If you feel a bit weak while you're there, faced with this wealth of riches, and all this reading, you can press yourself a bottle of fresh orange juice. And if you need to sit down, next door there's a little eating place, La Fabrique, which serves the products of the shop and every day offers a soup, a quiche, a main dish, a salad and a dessert. This is the way the world should be run!

Address 55 Rue Notre-Dame de Lorette, 75009 Paris, +33 (0)1 53 16 10 10. Also at 222 Rue Saint-Martin 75003 and 99 Rue Rambuteau, 75001 Paris | **Getting there** Métro to Notre-Dame-de-Lorette (Line 12); bus 26, 32, 43, 67 or 74 | **Hours** Mon–Sat 10am–9pm; restaurant Mon–Fri noon–3pm | **Tip** At the end of the street, in the middle of the charming Place Saint-Georges, stands an impressive fountain built in 1911 with, on top, a bust of the French illustrator Paul Gavarni and decorated round its base with characters from the Paris Carnival.

24_ La Cave de Belleville
The perfect cave à manger

A *cave à manger* is just what it sounds like – a wine cellar where you can eat. Created in 2015, this beautiful and vast cave à manger used to be a warehouse selling equipment for the leather industry, and many of the original fixtures and fittings have been kept and modernised in a very clever way. The place feels comfortably new and old at the same time. You sit on beautiful long wooden tables (seating between 40 and 50) under very elegant lighting and… well… drink, eat, chat and relax.

There's no real cooking or substantial kitchen – this is a cave à manger. You create your own meal from the many plates and dishes on offer. On the menu are varieties of seafood, such as scallops, mussels and razor shells, squid and octopus and sardines in olive oil. You can choose a small board or large, according to your appetite, of salami, Serrano ham or cheeses, plus a plate called The Prestige Iberico on which everything is Spanish. There's a choice between the warm tartine of the day (an open sandwich), or the vegetarian option, made with raw vegetables, or the salad of the day (when I went it was nectarine, fennel and Serrano), the burrata (a creamy mozzarella dish) to share, and the foie gras dish (according to the season). For dessert, there's a chocolate mousse or Greek yoghurt with fresh fruit.

The shop is at the front. They have an excellent cheese counter selling Corsican tomme, Camembert, Saint-Félicien, Manchego, mozzarella, burrata and scamorza. The charcuterie is stocked with dried, smoked and flavoured saucissons and farm-made Spanish preserves and chipirones (small squid cooked in ink). The wines – mainly organic and made with natural yeast – come from all over the world – Italy, Germany, Greece, Georgia, Spain and Portugal. And they also sell apple and pear ciders from the Domaine du Tertre, fruit juices, artisan beers and several spirits.

Address 51 Rue de Belleville, 75019 Paris, +33 (0)1 40 34 12 95 | **Getting there** Métro to Belleville (Line 2 or 11); bus 26, 48 or 60 | **Hours** Mon 5pm–midnight, Tue–Sat 10am–midnight, Sun 11.30am–6.30pm | **Tip** At no. 72 there is a plaque that marks the steps where the great singer Edith Piaf was born in 1915. They are still as they were.

25 La Cave des Papilles

Natural wines, without hangovers

Natural wines don't taste like ordinary wines because they are, in essence, a pure form of fermented grape juice, retaining the taste of the fruit. They're not only made from organic grapes grown without insecticides, weed killers and non-organic fertilisers, but they're also wines that are naturally fermented without chemical additives. The sulphides used in conventional wine production are either totally absent, or reduced to the absolute minimum. Everything in these wines is, therefore, digestible, with the result that they never leave you with that 'morning after' feeling.

Gérard Katz met Jean-Pierre Robinot, the extraordinary, radical winemaker, by chance in a bar in Paris in 1989 and was immediately converted to this modern / ancient form of viticulture. He opened Les Papilles in 1996, where you could eat delicious snacks and taste the many natural wines on offer. Then he opened La Cave des Papilles in 2001. *Papilles* is French for the tastebuds on the tongue.

His shop now lists wines from about 1,000 small-scale producers from around the world. Not all of these wines are available all of the time, of course, but the packed shelves and stacked floors give the impression that they are. The wines are all made by independent winemakers who ensure that their wines reflect the special characteristics of the localities where they're grown and made. Gérard Katz and his enthusiastic team know all about these wines, and you leave not just with new tastes to enjoy but also with new thoughts in your mind.

Gérard organises wine tastings every month, where his faithful clients can meet the winemakers themselves. The annual Fête des Papilles is usually held on the first Sunday in September, when the street is closed to traffic. It always attracts a huge crowd, musicians and singers perform throughout the day, and everyone drinks, eats and laughs a lot.

Address 35 Rue Daguerre, 75014 Paris, +33 (0)1 43 20 05 74 | Getting there Métro to Denfert-Rochereau (Line 4 or 6); bus 38, 68 or 88 | Hours Mon 3.30–8.30pm, Tue–Fri 10am–1.30pm & 3.30–8.30pm, Sat 10am–8.30pm, Sun 10am–1.30pm | Tip At 261 Boulevard Raspail, you can see the Fondation Cartier, designed by the architect Jean Nouvel, which shows thought-provoking exhibitions. The garden Theatrum Botanicum by Lothar Baumgarten is an example of nature in its raw state.

26 _ Chambelland
A shrine to a gluten-free world

Nathaniel Doboin and Thomas Teffri-Chambelland created Chambelland in 2014 to address the growing problem of modern gluten allergies. To do this they built their own flour mill in Haute-Provence and developed their own original recipes based on rice, sorghum and millet flours, which are naturally gluten-free. The raw materials they use, all from organic farms, are free from chemicals, and everything is cooked in their own ovens. Their control standards are impeccable, and they have been certified organic by Écocert.

The choice is enormous: a country loaf, a five-grain loaf, a 'bread of the athletes', bread with chocolate and a 'bread of the moment'. They make a plain focaccia and two others with herbs or olives, and two types of sweet bread with rice flour – one with orange flower and the other with candied orange peel and chocolate granules. They offer their own delicious granola, a mix of puffed rice, toasted buckwheat, hemp, sunflower and pumpkin seeds, raisins, cranberries, hazelnuts, coconut, cinnamon, salt, olive oil and honey. At the pâtisserie counter, among many delights, is a special chocolate and strawberry tart.

Their menu, called l'Humeur du Jour, varies according to the season. On offer when I was there were bruschetta, with tomato, rocket, olive and garlic, a creamy dip of roasted carrots, a vegetarian sandwich with fennel, ginger, carrots and orange and a meat sandwich with Bayonne ham, honey, mustard and salad. To drink they serve fruit juices, sparkling or still orangeade and lemonade, soya milk, teas and infusions, coffee and spiced chocolate. They also sell a few gluten-free recipe books, and the excellent cordials of the Belvoir Fruit Farms.

The whole place is immaculate, with a delightful terrace facing a little square with a village atmosphere that makes you feel you are miles from Paris, and from our modern world full of chemicals.

Address 14 Rue Ternaux, 75011 Paris, +33 (0)1 43 55 07 30 | **Getting there** Métro to Parmentier (Line 3); bus 46 or 96 | **Hours** Tue–Sat 8am–8pm, Sun 8am–6pm | **Tip** This ancient popular quarter of Paris is still full of lively and attractive bistros. Stroll along and discover…

27 — Chez Virginie
A place where cheese is loved

Keeping and maturing cheese is a rare skill. Virginie is one of the very few cheesemongers in Paris who still matures cheeses in her own cellars. She learned her skill from her father, who ran the *fromagerie* from 1946. Her shop is an absolute delight to visit. When I went there, twigs of little green apples hung above the racks of cheeses in the window and a few carefully placed, delicately tinted dahlias enlivened the display inside. But what makes this place special is the helpful labelling. Every cheese is neatly and very precisely described, with its name, whether it's made with cow's, sheep's or goat's milk, or a blend, with information, of course, about its origin, and the price. If you want to find out about cheeses, this is the place to learn – and Virginie is only too happy to impart her knowledge and enthusiasm.

The variety of cheeses on offer is impressive: most of the main French cheeses are represented, alongside a few curiosities such as the Délice de Pommard, a mustard husk, and Pommard cow cheese. She also stocks foreign cheeses: a matured Etivaz from Switzerland; mozzarella, burrata and Parmesan from Italy; Manchego from Spain; a smoked Cheddar from England marinated in whisky; a mature Gouda and aged Mimolette from Holland and a feta from the Greek island of Euboea. She also offers a few home-made dishes that change with the season: a truffle Brillat-Savarin (of international renown – says her label!), a Figou stuffed with figs, and a Parigot covered with fresh chives.

In addition, she sells an exquisitely selected range of dairy and grocery products: butter from Beurre Bordier, Le Fierbois yoghurts, gherkins and soup from the famous Maison Marc, the extraordinary burdock honeys of the Maison Hédène, piment d'Espelette paste, Pouilles pastas, Luscombe ginger beer, the famous Escuminac maple syrups… This is a place where food, and above all cheese, is loved.

- Fromage de brebis -

Le Figou

A la compotée de figue - Maison!

Lait cru - Fermier - MGNP

Prix à la pièce 7,95 €

Address 125 Rue Caulaincourt, 75018 Paris, +33 (0)1 42 58 14 57. Also at 54 Rue Damrémont, 75018 Paris | **Getting there** Métro to Lamarck-Caulaincourt (Line 12); bus 80 | **Hours** Tue 4–8pm, Wed–Sat 9.30am–1pm & 4–8pm, Sun 10am–1pm | **Tip** No. 21 was once one of the studios of Toulouse-Lautrec. Walk along the beautiful Avenue Junot, which leads up to the Butte Montmartre, and spot the plates on the houses where many artists lived.

28_CheZaline

Possibly the most delicious sandwiches in Paris

This very old, small horse-butcher's shop (you can still see the horse head sign above the door) has been converted by Delphine Zampetti into what has become one of the best sandwich and takeaway shops in Paris.

The list of *casse-croûte* (snacks) is announced at the entrance: 'Les classiques baguette tradition' comes with a choice of one or two ingredients: Prince de Paris ham or chorizo, Saint-Nectaire cheese or the blue cheese Fourme d'Ambert. Then follow 'Les cuisinés baguette tradition', made from cooked ingredients: chicken pot-au-feu with mayonnaise and salad; potato tortilla with chorizo; Prince de Paris ham with pesto and goat's cheese; piquillos (little stuffed peppers), tapenade, goat's cheese and salad; haddock with dill cream and pickled cabbage; beef axoa (a spicy stew) with tapenade and samphire. And then come 'Les cuisinés pain rond au sésame' (cooked dishes in a round sesame bun) such as: bonito with egg, tapenade, samphire and salad; Prince de Paris ham with guacamole and carrot; celeriac remoulade with Prince de Paris ham plus mayonnaise and salad. The desserts of the day were apple and apricot crumble, vanilla and lemon rice pudding.

In addition there's a whole range of dishes to take away: bonito *en escabèche* (a southern French way of cooking with stock); lentil, fennel and carrot salad; chicken pot-au-feu with vegetables and herbs; egg mimosa (a classic, delicious variant on the hard-boiled egg); tomato and samphire salad. To drink: their own freshly squeezed fruit and vegetable juices, Elixir lemonade and Philomenn beer from Brittany. There are a few stools along the counter, but from noon on there's always a queue. Hardly surprising because everything is delicious, fresh and affordable. As the French say, *et le tour est joué*, which literally means 'the game is up', that's to say if you're not happy with this you can just go home.

Address 85 Rue de la Roquette, 75011 Paris, +33 (0)1 43 71 90 75 | **Getting there**
Métro to Voltaire (Line 9); bus 61 or 69 | **Hours** Mon–Fri 11.30am–4pm | **Tip** The
Rue de la Roquette leads to Père Lachaise, Paris' largest and best known cemetery. It is
the final resting place of many famous people, including Balzac, Maria Callas, Camus,
Edith Piaf, Chopin, Colette, Proust, Oscar Wilde and Jim Morrison.

29 — Chocolaterie Cyril Lignac
The end of the road for chocoholics

Cyril Lignac is a household name in France. Only just turned 40, he's the chef and owner of a starred restaurant and his cookbooks have sold millions of copies. His TV appearances have made him even more famous, where his favourite comments '*c'est gourmand*' '*c'est croquant*' (untranslatable into English – literally meaning 'it's greedy', 'it's crunchy') have become catchphrases, so popular in fact that he's decided to use them as a brand name for his own products.

He opened La Chocolaterie in 2016, a shop / café almost totally dedicated to chocolate. Inside are a few tables and a table d'hôte (a large one for everyone) and outside an attractive little terrace. To drink, of course, there's hot and iced chocolate and the whole standard range of coffees. The chocolates and coffees come with or without Chantilly cream. They also serve orange juice, soft drinks and Earl Grey, Marco Polo or Fuji Yama teas.

To nibble: chocolatine, chocolate-caramel cookie, marbled loaf, tigré au chocolat, toochoco, caramel and orange flower brownies, chocolate flan, gianduja praline tarte, le Suisse (a cake as light as a soufflé), the quatre heures (a brioche stuffed with a very thin chocolate bar, a favourite of kids coming out of school, hence its name), and an ourson (a chocolate bear with marshmallow filling). A huge pyramid of 60 little bears stands on the counter, beside a few pastries, éclairs and chocolate cakes. Ranged along the walls are dozens of chocolate bars, made with different cacao brands, all elegantly wrapped, including ones with interesting flavours like caramelised almonds, sesame and green tea. The bonbons are filled chocolate squares that can be separated like sweets.

In front of the Chocolaterie you'll find Cyril Lignac's pâtisserie and round the corner his restaurant, Le Chardenoux, with its beautiful Art Nouveau décor, which is now listed as a historic monument.

Address 25 Rue Chanzy, 75011 Paris, +33 (0)1 55 87 21 40. Also at 34 Rue du Dragon, 75006 Paris | **Getting there** Métro to Faidherbe-Chaligny (Line 8) or Charonne (Line 9); bus 46, 56 or 76 | **Hours** Daily 8am–7pm | **Tip** At 30, Cité Prost you will find a building built by the architect Bernard Buhler, known for his imaginative use of colour. The old buildings there were demolished in 2006 and have been replaced by the attractive garden of Folie-Titon.

30__Le Comptoir de la Gastronomie

Abundance from the south west, before fridges

Le Comptoir de la Gastronomie dates back to a time when Les Halles was a great market, what Zola called the 'Belly of Paris'. A beautiful Art Nouveau façade, dating from 1894, invites the visitor into this exceptional shop and café/bar. The shelves and tables are so full of products that you have the impression you've walked into the old pantry of a country house, a pantry from before there were fridges.

There are hosts of prepared dishes in glass storage jars, most of them from the south west of France, which is the regional speciality of the Comptoir. Dishes such as cassoulet (a duck and bean casserole), quail with foie gras and piperade (a hot ratatouille). There are many types of canned food, including fish pâté and marinated octopus and, of course, foie gras, raw, half-cooked or canned. But pride of place goes to the famous Fondant Baulois of the Maison Marylou – a chocolate fudge and salted butter cake – not for the faint-hearted!

The restaurant has 30 seats, and an additional 20 on the terrace outside. The beauty about eating here is that you can eat as much or as little as you like, and get a real taste of the best quality food from the south west of France, without committing yourself to a full-blown meal in a restaurant. With that in mind, the menu offers Les Classiques du Comptoir – plates of half-cooked foie gras with chutney and toast; roasted duck breast with spices and mashed potatoes; a cassoulet with duck cooked with lard and snails from Bourgogne. They also offer a seasonal menu, with many seafood specialities. For dessert, there's a strawberry tart with Chantilly cream or a mi-cuit au chocolat, an individual cake, served warm, with a runny chocolate centre – just in case you feel in need of a few more calories. And they offer a huge range of delicious sandwiches, with different daily fillings, to take away. Here, abundance reigns.

Address 34 Rue Montmartre, 75001 Paris, +33 (0)1 42 33 31 32 | **Getting there** Métro to Les Halles (Line 4); bus 38 or 47 | **Hours** Mon 9am–8pm, Tue–Sat 8am–8pm; restaurant Mon–Thu noon–11pm, Fri & Sat noon–midnight | **Tip** Next door, the shop La Bovida sells professional cooking materials, spices and decorations, as does Mora just opposite. A bit further down, Simon offers the same services.

31__La Coop
The Alps at the gates of the Luxembourg Gardens

La Coop springs from an initiative begun by famers in 1957 in the Savoie region of France, particularly the Haute-Savoie (which includes the French Alps and Mont Blanc). They formed a collective to save their traditional mountain farming methods. The co-operative now includes 170 farmers who pool their milk to make their famous Beaufort cheese and sell it directly to customers, while maintaining their sustainable form of agriculture. They aren't at all backward looking, and are always looking out for new techniques. Hence the spruce, modern look of their shop in Paris, which sells their Beaufort cheese, alongside many other fine regional products.

The shop is impeccable and spacious, and offers many Savoy cheeses (tommes, bleus, reblochon, etc.), hand-churned butter and grated cheese. They also sell sausages: the Godiveau (veal and pork), the Diots de Savoie (pork and white wine), the Caillasse (dried and smoked pork fillet), the dried beef from Tarine and Abondance, the Ancelle (dried pork fillet), vacuum-packed veal (both escalopes and cuts for a stew), saucisson sec with boletus mushrooms, all from Savoy.

In addition, they stock artisanal lemonade; beer from the Mont Blanc brewery; roussette (a delicious dry white wine); a liqueur de génépi (wormwood); wild rose hip, plum, blackberry and raspberry jams; fruit purée (apple / blueberry); honeys; crozets (small rectangular pasta); cooked dishes in jars such as terrines (with wild garlic or Beaufort cheese)... you can almost smell the mountain air before you taste them.

One table in the shop and more in the vaulted cellar downstairs enable you to enjoy the delights of the Bar à Fromages, with a choice of boards (cheeses, charcuterie or both) and wine by the glass from a self-service dispenser, operated, with typical modernity, by a card you get from the counter. The excellent bread comes from Émile & Jules.

Address 9 Rue Pierre Corneille, 75006 Paris, +33 (0)1 43 29 91 07 | Getting there Métro to Odéon (Line 4 or 10); bus 38 | Hours Mon–Sat 11am–8.30pm, Sun 2.30–7.30pm | Tip The Palais du Luxembourg across the road, built by Marie de' Medici in 1612, is the seat of the French Senate and you can visit it when the senators are not sitting (for times check on the website www.senat.fr).

32   Courty et Fils
The cutting edge for cooking

It's a law of gardening that you can't trim plants properly unless you use the right tools. Plants flourish if they're skilfully pruned. As the gardener's saying goes: 'growth follows the knife.' The same is true of cooking. The flavours of meat and fish, fruit and vegetables are released if the joints and fillets, slices and segments are properly cut. But you can only do this if you have the right knives. I love them; they're the cook's second hand: little knives for cutting small things like shallots and garlic; a big strong knife for slicing a roast and another more pointed one for carving meat off bones; a fine one for chopping onions and herbs; a long, very thin blade for filleting fish as finely as possible. Buy three good knives and a sharpening steel and you'll be happy in the kitchen for the rest of your life.

Courty is the great knife shop of Paris. The choice is enormous. They have knives from all over France as well as foreign ones including fabulous Japanese blades. They stock all traditional cutlery, artisanal craft knives and even second-hand and some antique blades. They sell blades for all uses, including shaving. The place is almost a museum of knives, and the staff behind the counter are world experts.

All the famous brands are represented: Opinel, Laguiole, Victor Inox, the renowned Durandal, made in ceramic, the rustic and hard wearing Douk Douk created in 1929 for the Far Eastern and Oceanic markets.

Among my favourites, I'd like to mention Perceval from Thiers, the Sheffield of France. They are expensive but exceptional. They make tableware, folding pocket knives, kitchen knives, carving, slicing and chopping knives. They're all forge-beaten and have razor-sharp edges. Their sharpening steels are absolutely exceptional – just a few strokes bring the blades back to perfection. You can also leave your knives here for sharpening.

Address 44 Rue des Petits Champs, 75002 Paris, +33 (0)1 42 96 59 21 | **Getting there** Métro to Pyramides (Line 7); bus 29, 39, 48 or 67 | **Hours** Mon–Sat 9.30am–7pm | **Tip** At no. 45, on the corner with Rue Sainte-Anne, you will find the Hôtel Lully built in 1670 for the famous Baroque composer Jean-Baptiste Lully, court composer to Louis XIV. The façade facing Rue Sainte-Anne is ornamented with bas-reliefs of musical instruments.

33 __ Crus et Découvertes

The new grands crus of natural wine

'Cru' has no direct equivalent in English – it means, roughly, a vintage from a particular locality. Mikael Lemasle became passionate about natural wines and decided to open his little but very welcoming shop in 2005. It is full – literally packed to the rafters – with discoveries. There are no fewer than 350 different wines on sale here many from vintages that have become famous in the natural wine world. Here you will find Fanny Sabre Bourgogne, Loire wines made by Brendan Tracey, Olivier Lemasson and Jean-Pierre Robinot, wines of the Ardèche made by Gilles Azzoni, Languedoc wines, such as Axel Prüfer's Le Temps des Cerises or Jean-François Nicq's Les Foulards Rouges, Jura wines made by Jean-Baptiste Ménigoz and the Domaine de l'Octavin, and Alsace wines by Binner, which are sold together with his fruit spirits. Once tasted, never forgotten. The shop looks beyond the French borders to Italy, Spain, Germany, Austria and Georgia, where they still make a macerated wine kept in amphoras, which give it a slightly almond taste. They even have a Pinot Noir from Oregon, in the United States.

Mikael Lemasle also stocks whiskies, rums and vodkas, farm-made ciders and beers, including a very light IPA and a beer from the Brasserie des Vignes de Gaillac, which is brown and flowery. The epicerie section is small, selling sardines from the Compagnie Bretonne, excellent saucissons sec from Chavassieux and the scrumptious ice creams of La Tropicale, such as coconut and sesame, yoghurt and thyme, and ginger and caramel.

A little bit further along the street are the twin Paul Bert and À l'Écailler du Paul Bert restaurants (the latter specialising in seafood) offering an imaginative re-visiting of traditional French cuisine, using only seasonal products. After a wine tasting at Crus et Découvertes, these are perfect places to finish the evening.

Address 7 Rue Paul Bert, 75011 Paris, +33 (0)1 43 71 56 79 | **Getting there** Métro to Charonne (Line 9); bus 46, 56 or 76 | **Hours** Mon 4–8pm, Tue–Thu 10.30am–1pm & 4–8pm, Fri 10.30am–1.30pm & 3.30–8.30pm, Sat 10.30am–8.30pm | **Tip** At 37 bis Rue de Montreuil, the Cour de l'Industrie is a cluster of lodgings and workshops dating back to the 19th century, with a paved yard, now a listed historic monument.

34__Dada

Down to earth with eyes on heaven

In the heart of Paris' 'Vegitown', fruit, vegetables and herbs of irreproachable freshness are enthroned under a majestic white dome of light, more familiar in a church or mosque. To the sides, elegant shelves from floor to ceiling strain under the weight of groceries, drinks, cosmetics and therapeutic aids. Dada boasts an exceptional range of foods suitable for all allergies. It is famed for the helpfulness and expertise of its staff who alone make a visit here a unique experience. A slightly surprising aspect is the presence of meat and charcuterie, albeit in refrigerated glass cases. Dada is nothing if not pragmatic – after all it has to survive in the middle of Paris – but its purity of presentation and approach reveals, one suspects, its ultimate agenda: the death of meat. The future partner of mankind is the vegetable.

There is a religious awe about the whole experience. When you enter, the first thing you see, on the right, is a counter selling bread and wine – the fundamental food of the Bible. On the left, there is a tempting display of takeaway delicacies – selected, one feels, with missionary zeal. The wealth of choices is almost embarrassing: hot curries and risottos, soups, sandwiches, savoury tarts, fresh juices and smoothies, as well as exquisite sweets, cookies and muffins – every morsel personally approved by chef Julie Basset, one of the high priestesses of French vegetarian cuisine.

Dada upholds the standards of the Biocoop movement, by respecting producers, taking responsibility for quality, only selling products that are 100 per cent organic and in season.

The shop was created by Yannick Le Bourgeois and Marie-Laure Dumarché in 2015, who, with the architect Jeff Van Dyck, converted the horses' entrance yard to an old private town house, fitting it with a beautiful dome – creating the ultimate shrine to the vegetable.

Address 29 Rue de Paradis, 75010 Paris, +33 (0)1 40 79 43 51 | Getting there Métro to Château d'Eau (Line 4); bus 38, 39 or 47 | Hours Mon–Fri 10am–8pm, Sat 10am–8.30pm, Sun 10am–1pm | Tip At 18 Rue de Paradis you can see the fancy façade of the previous Faïencerie de Choisy-le-Roi – a glimpse of 19th-century decorative splendour.

35 Desnoyer and Co
Quality from meadow to table

After 15 years in the 14th Arrondissement as a renowned butcher, Hugo Desnoyer wanted a bigger place with tables where people could try his produce as well as buy it. He bought a former butcher's shop in the 16th Arrondissement, and with the architect Alain Baudouin, realised his dream: a meat counter with an adjacent, informal 20-seat bistro where customers can choose what they want to eat from the display and Hugo's team cooks it for them on the spot! There is a basic, simple menu of grilled steak, roasted bone marrow, egg mayonnaise, rib chop and calves' liver. He also has an organic vegetable garden in Mayenne to provide all the vegetables and fruit.

Hugo Desnoyer's career was a love story from the start. He had hated school so much that his frustrated father gave him two options: to work as a carpenter or as a butcher. He loved working with wood, but the silky feel of meat thrilled him even more. Cheekily, he chose to open his first butcher's shop on 1 April, 1998, with the enthusiastic support of Chris, his wife and business partner. The Saturday queue became a favourite meeting place for his customers, who enjoyed the banter with his loyal staff. Manuel Martinez, then chef of the prestigious Tour d'Argent, spotted Hugo's talent and suddenly all doors opened for him.

The secret of Hugo's success is the quality of his meat. He knows everything about the animals and their breeders. His favourite locality in France is Charente Limousine where the cattle are reared on grasslands without pesticides and fertilisers, and fed, in their last year, with secret, organic nutrients. They are killed in small, family-run abattoirs, which take special care of their animals. It comes as no surprise that Hugo was the first butcher to be listed in the international *Who's Who* and in 2017 the Japanese broadcasting channel NHK World named him the best butcher in the world.

Address 28 Rue du Docteur Blanche, 75016 Paris, +33 (0)1 46 47 83 00. Also at 45 Rue Boulard, 75014 Paris, +33 (0)1 45 40 76 67 | **Getting there** Métro to Jasmin or Ranelagh (Line 9); bus 22 | **Hours** Tue–Sat 8.30am–7.30pm, Sun 8am–1pm; table d'hôtes: Tue–Sat 11.30am–3.30pm | **Tip** At 8–10 Square du Docteur Blanche there is the Maison La Roche, a rare survivor of a 1920s house designed by the famous French architects Le Corbusier and Pierre Jeanneret. Walk back into a Modernist past!

36 Du Pain et des Idées

Bread as it used to be

Christophe Vasseur, after a career in fashion, turned his attention to bread. His idea was simple and ambitious: to return bread to its central place in people's diet by using only the best natural ingredients and traditional hand-making methods to bring out all its flavours. His aim was to make bread, as he likes to say, 'full of love and friendship.'

His emblematic loaf is called Le Pain des Amis and is now served in many of the best restaurants in Paris. It's made with only a pinch of yeast and very little kneading but it's left to rise over two days, giving it a chestnut and maple syrup flavour, with a magnificent thick crust. His standard loaves are made daily with wheat, buckwheat or chestnut flour and natural yeast. On Thursdays, a rye loaf is added, and on Tuesdays and Fridays extra loaves are made with roasted cereals, and occasionally with walnut and hazelnut, ginger and maple syrup, honey and grain mustard. On Fridays, they offer the Incredible Rabelais (named after the bawdy French writer) – a scrumptious brioche made with chestnut honey, saffron, turmeric and walnuts from the Périgord.

The bakery makes a few delicious traditional extras – an apple turnover in flaky pastry, a Danish pastry with lemon and nougat or chocolate and pistachio, and the Mouna, a brioche flavoured with orange blossom. The butter comes from organic farms, and the water is filtered to eliminate unpleasant chemicals. Everything sold in the bakery is cooked on the spot, on stone, not metal, which gives all its products their very special taste.

In 2002, Christophe Vasseur found his dream location – an old bakery dating back to 1870, which had kept its beautiful façade and interior, preserved as a historic monument. Christophe Vasseur could be on the way to becoming one himself, for the celebrated Gault & Millau named him Best Baker of Paris in 2008.

Address 34 Rue Yves Toudic, 75010 Paris, +33 (0)1 42 40 44 52 | **Getting there** Métro to République (Line 3, 5, 8, 9 or 11); bus 56, 65 or 75 | **Hours** Mon–Fri 7am–8pm | **Tip** The Canal Saint-Martin, next door, with its beautiful bridges, provides a delightful place to walk along the water's edge.

37 __ E. Dehillerin

An Aladdin's cave for cooks

Coming in off the bright street, your eyes take a little while to get accustomed to the lofty, old-fashioned, dark interior of Dehillerin's. Then, slowly, you begin to realise you've entered a fascinating cave of treasures. Every surface is covered with intriguing objects, some made of shining copper and brass, steel and glass glinting in the half-light. Many hang from the ceilings and down the walls, or are ranged along dark shelves or in trays of boxes on top of old cabinets stacked with drawers.

Everything a cook could dream of using is here: from the simplest knives and wooden spatulas to the most sophisticated cake, terrine and jelly moulds, in the form of all manner of shapes and creatures; from basic stacks of cooking pans, to elaborate skillets, cocottes, enamelled cast-iron pots, casseroles and griddles; all sizes of pestles and mortars, sieves and graters, whisks and mincers. And among them all are elaborate, specialist items like the duck presses used to screw the last drop of juice out of the carcass used to make the famous Canard au Sang, an emblematic recipe of the famous restaurant La Tour d'Argent. For Dehillerin is the haunt not just of amateur cooking enthusiasts but also of the most sophisticated chefs in France.

La Maison Dehillerin, in the middle of the quartier des Halles, rapidly became famous as a specialist service to French gastronomy when it was first founded in 1820. The shop is distinguished not only by the extraordinary range of its stock but also for the quality of its tools and utensils, many of which are sourced from small-scale craft suppliers. Dehillerin's reputation soon spread abroad. In 1912, the shop supplied some of the cooking equipment for the *Titanic*, but of course these went down with the ship. The American chef and television star, Julia Child, often frequented Dehillerin, and made it famous in the USA.

Address 18 and 20 Rue Coquillère, 75001 Paris, +33 (0)1 42 36 53 13 | **Getting there** Métro to Les Halles (Line 4); bus 67, 74 or 85 | **Hours** Mon 9am–12.30pm & 2–6pm, Tue–Fri 9am–7pm, Sat 9am–6pm | **Tip** Visit the beautiful garden of the Palais Royal and gaze up at the window of the flat where the famous writer Colette lived.

38_ L'Éclair de Génie

Eclairs of genius with amazing flavours

Christophe Adam enjoyed an exemplary career in the pâtissierie world: he started very young in Quimper, then worked with Christophe Felder at the Crillon Palace Hotel. His reputation grew and he became chef at Palace Hotel Beaurivage in Lausanne. In 1996, he started work at Fauchon where he became Chef Pâtissier in 2001. Some 15 years later he felt sufficiently in control of his art to open his own business establishing, in 2012, L'Éclair de Génie Rue Pavée, where he was at last able to give free reign to his own special creativity.

His eclairs are famous for their amazing flavours: caramel and salted butter, praline and almond, vanilla and pecan, passion fruit and raspberry, 72 per cent Araguani dark chocolate, yuzu lemon with meringue, rose and lychee, mascarpone and wild strawberries, apricot cheesecake… and there are always new flavours, changing with the seasons. L'Éclair de Génie offers also macarons and viennoiseries. You can sit at a table at the back of the shop, in a cosy ambiance, for a coffee, a tea, a chocolate, a capuccino (with precise origins always given on the menu) or a fresh fruit cocktail. They serve an assortment of sweet or savoury dishes, such as a Croque Vivienne – a refined version of the croque-monsieur – which comes with salad and vegetable crisps. They are always revamping their salads according to the season. To finish, they offer a café gourmand, ice cream, a sorbet or a fruit salad. On Sundays you can brunch on a more than generous menu.

L'Éclair de Génie now has 10 outlets in Paris and shops in Hong Kong, Milan, Moscow, Vancouver, Tbilisi and Qatar. Christophe Adam also has a restaurant, Le Dépôt Légal, at 6 Rue des Petits Champs, open seven days a week, which offers lively fresh cuisine as well as selling their grocery products, like Crapottes (caramelised puff pastry sticks) and their whole range of chocolate bars.

Address 14 Rue Pavée, 75004 Paris (original shop), +33 (0)1 84 79 23 40 | **Getting there** Métro to Saint-Paul (Line 1); bus 29, 69, 76 or 96 | **Hours** Daily 11am–7.30pm | **Tip** At no. 24, the Hôtel d'Angoulême Lamoignon, built at the end of the 16th century, now houses the Bibliothèque Historique de la Ville de Paris, which is open to the public, specialising in the history of Paris and the Île-de-France.

39__Émile & Jules

For the love of bread

The Winacour family has run the Moulin des Moissons farm since the 19th century. When many farms faced closure, Marc Winacour decided to diversify by establishing a mill to grind his own flour and a bakery to bake his own bread. He revived traditional methods, using grinding stones that preserve all the flavours of the grain. His eldest son, Émile, after studying at catering college, took over the bakery, making uniquely flavoured bread by blending different grains. The youngest son, Jules, then joined the enterprise, selling the family's bread in local markets. He was so successful that Émile and Jules decided to open their first shop in Paris in the 17th Arrondissement. Traceability and locality proved of great appeal to their customers. The family could prove where everything in their bread came from, and their farm was less than 50 kilometres from Paris.

The star product of Émile and Jules is l'Oreiller, a real 'pain de campagne', which you can keep for five days. You'll also find the traditional baguette here, called l'Épi – the ear of the wheat – which comes with pavot – poppy seeds, sesame seeds or ginger. If you fancy a brioche for breakfast, you have a choice between a natural plain one, or others with fruit or white chocolate.

The shop is busiest at lunchtime, when the team make sandwiches to order on the spot, which you can eat at the tables or take away. Le Mixte comes with ham, Emmental, butter and romaine lettuce. Le Thon comes with home-made tuna mousse, cherry tomatoes and lamb's lettuce. Le Chorizo comes with bellotta pork, Corsican sheep's cheese, butter and romaine lettuce. Le Grison comes with dried Grison meat from Switzerland, Comté, piment d'Espelette butter and romaine lettuce. You have the choice between four different breads, one being a delicious focaccia made partly with wholemeal flour. Bread's the business at Émile & Jules.

Brioche au chocolat
noir
5,90 €   450gr

Brioche à
l'ancienne
5,00 €   450gr

Brioch
écorces
et fleur
5,

Address 2 Rue Vavin, 75006 Paris, +33 (0)1 73 75 67 44. Also at 18 Rue de la Terrasse, 75017 Paris | **Getting there** Métro to Vavin (Line 4); bus 68 or 83 | **Hours** Mon–Sat 8am–8pm | **Tip** The handsome Luxembourg Garden, inspired by the Boboli Gardens in Florence at the initiative of Marie de' Médicis, which covers 25 hectares, and its museum, are just a few steps away.

40 Épicerie Roots
A market garden on the street

Walking down the Rue Leon Front, I was surprised to see tomatoes and herbs growing wildly in two big planters beside a rustic bench. I entered the shop behind and was enchanted. Fruit and vegetables, richly fragrant, filled many boxes, and at the counter there was a small but perfect selection of grocery products, wines and beverages.

Caroline and Maxime, the founders, immediately welcomed me. Both of them started their careers as cooks, working in Michelin-star restaurants, but turned instead to their main love, horticulture. They opened a market garden near Paris on permaculture, organic principles (developed in the late 1970s in Australia). Their next step was to open a shop in Paris where they could sell their own produce along with that of other market gardens that followed the same exacting principles.

Roots sells farm butter from Normandy, cheeses, flours, lentils, pasta, La Salorge sea salt, chickpeas, coquillettes (tiny twists of pasta loved by children), their own home-made jams and fruit juices including bissap (a beverage made with hibiscus flowers) and a delicious lemonade, which I tasted, all from the Atelier de la Pepie, as well as artisan beers and organic and natural wines. And from 4.30pm they sell the bread of the excellent baker Le Bricheton, in Rue de la Reunion.

Then their love for cooking came back – making takeaways: every day a different soup (cucumber and fresh mint gazpacho when I was there), a salad and a choice of three croque-monsieur: the Roots (Prince de Paris ham, with Mornay sauce and Emmental); the Fumé (smoked ham, Mornay sauce, Morbier cheese from the Jura and honey mustard) and the Vege (home-made tomato sauce, pesto, grilled courgette and burrata). For dessert, they offer clafoutis (a traditional baked fruit flan). Delicious. But if you sit on the bench outside to eat, take care, as it has a tendency to tip.

Address 47 Rue Léon Frot, 75011 Paris | **Getting there** Métro to Charonne (Line 9); bus 56 or 76 | **Hours** Tue–Fri 11am–2pm & 4.30–9pm, Sat 10am–9pm | **Tip** Go and enjoy your croque-monsieur in the charming Square Colbert at 159 Rue de Charonne. You need to push the gate of the buildings to enter – accessible during the daytime.

41 Épices Roellinger

A modern spice adventurer

Olivier Roellinger was born in Cancale in Brittany, near St Malo, where his family loved to entertain. After a rollicking youth, involving motorbikes, sailing, a few painful accidents, while studying chemistry and maths, he eventually settled down to become a cook. After studying with some of France's finest chefs, he opened his own restaurant, with his wife, Jane, in the family home on the Brittany coast, Les Maisons de Bricourt. He'd found his form of self-expression: the creation of exquisite flavours. He realised that these came, above all, from the basic ingredients. So he established close relationships with local fishermen, oyster cultivators, market gardeners and cattle breeders, developing dishes specially to bring out local flavours. His superb cuisine earned him three Michelin stars. But he was always searching for new horizons.

He became fascinated with the East India Company, which had introduced oriental tastes to Europe two centuries before. This stirred in him a new passion: spices. He created his first spice mix, called Retour des Indes, associating it enthusiastically with the sea and local products of his native Brittany. He then decided to travel the world with his wife to find the finest spices. He discovered that people rarely used only one spice, but a mix between 3 and as many as 20 different flavours.

Back home, Les Maisons de Bricourt became his laboratory and spice workshop, where he searched for new flavours, a bit like perfumes, with every powder meant for a precise dish. His rigorously selected spices are steamed, grilled, ground, pulverised, weighed, separated into portions and then mixed, to obtain his now famous blends, which are sold at his shop. There are so many, it's a bit overwhelming at first, but it's impossible not to find one that you really love. If you're lost, the excellent staff will be happy to guide you, by the nose.

Address 51 bis Rue Sainte-Anne, 75002 Paris, +33 (0)1 42 60 46 88 | **Getting there** Métro to Quatre-Septembre (Line 3); bus 7, 14, 39 or 68 | **Hours** Tue–Fri 10am–7pm, Sat 10am–6pm | **Tip** The Bibliothèque Nationale de France – Site Richelieu Louvois at 58 Rue de Richelieu – was the first national library in France to preserve printed heritage. The remarkable site, which has just been restored, shelters unique collections of manuscripts, iconography, maps, plans and prints, and organises wonderful exhibitions of world interest.

42 La Felicità

Italy on a grand scale

This is a triumph of imagination over scepticism. Tigrane Seydoux and Victor Lugger started their catering group in 2015. Despite all the detractors and the envious, they've gone from strength to strength. OK, you have to queue at La Felicità. OK, it's immense. OK, you have to spend a bit of money – it's not cheap, but it's certainly not expensive. But I have to say I am among the many who've been blown away, because, quite simply, this place is great fun and the food is great too.

In three short years, Tigrane and Victor have built an empire, opening six more places in Paris: East Mamma, Ober Mamma, Mamma Primi, Big Love Caffè, Popolare and Pink Mamma (I recommend them all). La Felicità is installed at the end of an old SNCF dispatch centre, built in the 1920s. The Halle Freyssinet (named after its constructor) is a feat of engineering, with a remarkable roof-span. It's a bit far from everything and difficult to find at first, but when you're there it's fun, lively, noisy and great.

Between the container trees and two trains, are six *bars à manger*: Il Gran Aperitivo serves risotto; La Trattoria serves mozzarella, burrata and pasta with seafood; there's an excellent burger bar; at another, 100 per cent organic pizzas are cooked before your eyes in a wood oven by a band of young Italian enthusiasts; La Grande Griglia serves T-bone steak, a quarter of roast chicken or barbecue ribs; Le Panificio offers salads and paninis. There are stands serving exciting desserts, seasonal fruit tarts, chocolate mousse, tiramisu, panna cotta, brownies, ice creams and milkshakes. There's an impressive cocktail bar, a Biergarten, a caffeteria with pancakes, delicious coffees and freshly squeezed fruit juices. And, in addition, there's a library and a concert venue. The staff are exceptionally efficient and friendly. And if you want to avoid queuing, you can order on their app.

Address 55 Boulevard Vincent Auriol, 75013 Paris | **Getting there** Métro to Chevaleret (Line 6); bus 27 | **Hours** Mon & Tue 12.15–2.30pm, Wed 12.15–2.30pm & 6–10.30pm, Thu & Fri 12.15–2.30pm & 6–11pm, Sat noon–11pm, Sun noon–10.30pm | **Tip** Le Quai de la Gare leads to the Bibliothèque Nationale de France François-Mitterrand, built by Dominique Perrault, and opened in 1996. It contains all the royal collections built up since the Middle Ages and holds exhibitions (for details visit their website www.bnf.fr).

43 La Ferme d'Alexandre

A dairy farm shop in the heart of Paris

Alexandre Pignol's great-grandfather ran a dairy farm in Surgères, in the Charente-Maritime. In 1979, his father expanded the family business by selling dairy products in markets. Then, in 2014, Alexandre took the next step and opened his first cheese shop in Paris. He sells cheeses selected from farmers and cheese maturers who share his respect for traditional cheese making.

There are about 300 cheeses on offer, made with raw or pasteurised milk. Among the famous cheeses of France and Europe are many rarities: l'Herve, a rather strong Belgian soft cheese with a washed crust; the Bethmale, an uncooked, pressed cheese with small holes – a rare product from the Pyrénées Ariégeoises; the Fumaison d'Auvergne, a delicious sheep's cheese; a glorious Gorgonzola served by the spoonful in season, and an impressive selection of goat's cheeses such as Persillé from the Yvelines, Racotin and Clacbitou from Burgundy, Brique de Ribière from the Auvergne, and Mothais on chestnut leaves.

The shop also makes its own specialities: Fontainebleau, a delicious combination of fromage blanc and whipped cream, which is ideal served as a starter with salt, pepper, dill and salmon or just as good as a dessert with a fruit coulis; a cider, apple and hazelnut Camembert and, in season, fresh goat's cheeses flavoured with apricot or grapes. For dessert you have a choice between speculoos and raspberry tiramisu, a chocolate pear charlotte or a chocolate mousse. I also recommend the Le Fierbois yoghurts, Basque curdled milk Ekia, and an excellent butter of the Fontaine des Veuves from Poitou-Charentes. For Christmas, he offers a remarkable cheese plate where the truffle rules supreme. He also has a delicatessen counter loaded with delights like L'épicurien jams, thyme syrup, caviar butter, sturgeon rillettes with caviar, gâche (a big, rich and soft brioche) and excellent wines.

Address 21 Rue Mouton Duvernet, 75014 Paris, +33 (0)1 45 39 18 63. Also at 19 Rue Saint Placide, 75006 Paris | **Getting there** Métro to Mouton Duvernet (Line 4); bus 38 | **Hours** Tue–Fri 9.30am–1.30pm & 4–8pm, Sat 9.30am–7.30pm | **Tip** Beside the Parc Montsouris there is a delightful corner of five cobbled streets bordered with beautiful houses where the famous artist Georges Braque had his studio.

44__Flora Danica
From the fields of Denmark to the Champs

The Champs-Élysées is called 'Les Champs' by the French, which translates as 'the fields'. This used to be the most exclusive shopping street in Paris, and the furthest from the countryside you could possibly get. Now it includes familiar high-street brands. Flora Danica is one of the truly unique treasures that remain and it's not at all exclusive, but friendly and lively, a real Danish brasserie. It was created in 1999 and a new interior installed by the Danish design team Gam-Fratesi. It's named after a wonderful set of prints of all the flowers from the fields of Denmark itself.

At the entrance, the shop sells Nordic specialities: herrings in dill or cumin, in spices or curry; dill-marinated salmon in thick slices named after the famous French singer Gilbert Bécaud (who really loved this dish); smoked eel and halibut; sweet and sour marinated cucumbers; potato salad with gravlax salmon and traditional smørrebrød (sliced rye bread) with salted mackerel. The drinks include detox juice of the Kookabarra company or, if you want to lose your mind, six varieties of Aquavits flavoured with aromatic herbs (meadow cumin/citruses; yellow fruits/cumin/black pepper; aniseed/coriander/lemon; black pepper/citruses/ginger; fennel/spices; and red berries/angostura) – fire juice from the fields in the back of your throat. For those with a sweet tooth, the desserts include tarts of all types – made with lemon, pistachio and cranberry, chocolate and strawberry and almond – fromage blanc with home-made muesli and Æblekage (stewed apples/redcurrants with whipped cream and macarons).

You can eat at the fine green marble counter or in the restaurant at the back, which opens onto a beautiful interior terrace, one of the hidden gardens of the Champs. The menu, conceived by the famous Danish chef Andreas Møller, with Leandro De Seta, specialises in smoked and marinated fish.

Address 142 Avenue des Champs-Élysées, 75008 Paris, +33 (0)1 44 13 86 26 | **Getting there** Métro to Charles de Gaulle-Étoile (Line 1, 2 or 6); bus 30, 52 or 73 | **Hours** Daily 8am–11.30pm | **Tip** At no.133 you can find the Publicis Drugstore, the first American-style drugstore that opened in France, in October 1958, and totally changed shopping across Europe.

45 Le Foyer de la Madeleine

Food for the soul against waste

The Madeleine, in the heart of one of the wealthiest districts in Paris, was originally built as a Greek temple to celebrate the glorious victories of Napoleon's army, but it was later turned into a church. Abbé Edouard Turgis opened the crypt to provide poor shop assistants working in the area with a place to have lunch. The Foyer is now run as a charity restaurant, open to all. More than 300 meals are served between noon and 2pm, thanks to 120 volunteers and 8 professional staff. The place is underground but surprising. Lamps designed by Philippe Starck float like clouds along the long, vaulted corridors. The menu is simple but tasty. You have a choice of starters and two main dishes – for example, tomato and basil soup followed by curried chicken or braised ham and port sauce, served with creamy spinach and French fries.

What makes Le Foyer exceptional is the incredible project of Massimo Bottura. With Lara Gilmore, he founded Food for Soul – which fights against food waste. The idea was to create meals for people facing hardship made by high-level cooks solely with surplus produce that would have otherwise been thrown away by shops. 'The Madeleine was a dream,' says Massimo Botturo. 'Look – under the crypt of a classified church we serve 100 meals a day from Monday to Friday, with 130 kilos of produce provided free every day and 40 volunteers.' Many of the most famous chefs in France took part in the project, including Yannick Alleno, Alain Ducasse, Olivier Roellinger, Anne-Sophie Pic, Pascal Barbot, Michel Troisgros, Alain Passard, Bertrand Grebaut, Jean-Francois Piege… producing delicious dinners out of waste while not in any way diminishing their reputations.

Le Foyer restaurant and professional kitchen can be rented for events, workshops or cooking lessons, with all profits going to the charity, but the evening meals are only open to those in need.

Address Église de la Madeleine, Place de la Madeleine, 75008 Paris (under the church in the crypt), +33 (0)1 47 42 39 84 | **Getting there** Métro to Madeleine (Line 8, 12 or 14); bus 24, 42, 52, 84 or 94 | **Hours** Mon–Fri 11.45am–2pm, no reservations | **Tip** Visit the Madeleine Church, the imposing monument to Napoleon's army, built in the neoclassical style. The organ, constructed by the illustrious Aristide Cavaillé-Coll, was played by both Camille Saint-Saëns and Gabriel Fauré.

46 __ G. Detou
Unbelievably everything

Detou means *de tout* in French, which translates as 'everything'. Here you will find literally every dried or preserved ingredient you need for pâtisserie and cuisine, and, for the most part, sold retail at wholesale prices. Here home cooks and professional chefs rub shoulders to buy what they need. Created in 1951 by Gérard Detou, the shop is virtually unchanged since then, except that it's now acquired an old-fashioned period charm. The wooden shelves are kept packed from floor to ceiling with products and the space to move between them is constricted, but don't worry – you'll be happy searching along them, like everyone else.

Hundreds of products invite you to pick them – from 'pistols' of chocolate in big bags or boxes (flakes, beads and shavings used by professional cake makers), tonka beans, dried fruits, nuts of all kinds, packets of glacé fruits and fruits in syrup, bottled and tinned fruit, coulis and purées, vanilla in all its forms (in pods, liquids, powder), sugar paste, almond, hazelnut, pistachio and praline pastes, all different types of edible colouring, spices, fondants (sugar preparations for cake icing), edible decorations of all colours and shapes, from sugar pearls to dainty ducks, wedding couples to Happy Birthday letters, bouquets of flowers, baskets of fruit and chocolate pearls, honeys, jams, spreads for tartine, gelatines, flours. In a word, all you need to add the finishing touches to the perfect cake.

Detou also stocks savoury and sour products: mustards, gherkins, vinegars, oils, sardines, preparations for stocks, foie gras and dried mushrooms.

The service can be a bit irregular, going from very nice to a bit grumpy, depending on the time of day, but it's always professional. And everyone expects you to spend a long time looking. But it's best to avoid the shop on Saturdays – it's so busy that moving about is almost impossible.

Address 58 Rue Tiquetonne, 75002 Paris, +33 (0)1 42 36 54 67 | **Getting there** Métro to Étienne Marcel (Line 4); bus 29 | **Hours** Mon–Sat 8.30am–6.30pm | **Tip** Take a stroll in the new Jardin Nelson Mandela around Les Halles, with playgrounds and lawns where you can lie down and relax.

47 __ GAG
Much more than a gag

It's a relief to come across GAG in the serious world of Parisian eco cuisine. GAG is short for Gras (fat), Alcool, Gluten – three forbidden tastes in the healthy Garden of Eden. It was created by Arnaud Daguin, cook, Alain Coumont, founder of Le Pain Quotidien and Roland Feuillas, a miller and baker. They like to say that GAG is *la vitrine du vivant* – it opens a window onto real life.

The shop in the front sells the bread made by Roland Feuillas himself. He says his gluten is healthy (and tasty) because it comes from old varieties of wheat and only natural yeasts. One of the greasiest fowls is a duck, and GAG sells duck liver pâté, duck rillettes and crisp duck scratchings (remains, including skin, cooked for a long time, deliciously, in fat). GAG sells Kintoa black pudding (made from Basque pigs), Corsican andouillette (sausage made with guts) and chorizo from the black pigs of Bigorre, and scrumptious raw butter from the Baratte du Crémier.

To the rear, in the restaurant, stands, enthroned, a Berkel, the great Rolls-Royce of all meat slicers. There you can enjoy the mouthwatering dishes of Arnaud Daguin. The menu changes according to the season, so I can only give a few examples. For starters, they offer a plate of Kintoa ham, roasted vegetables with two-herb mayonnaise and a mackerel brandade (a dish from Nîmes) with celery. The main dishes include lukewarm gravlax salmon with mashed potatoes, or toasted bread, smoked eel and celeriac remoulade, or gnochetti with wild mushroom sauce and grated aged sheep's cheese. For dessert there's strawberries with sugar or a coconut-milk espuma with a dash of Armagnac, warm bread and butter pudding with tangerine butter, and clafoutis with almond cream and almonds. And of course, natural wine, as much as you want. Glorious healthy living indeed, for those lucky not to suffer from any modern allergies.

Address 3 Rue de Palestro, 75002 Paris, +33 (0)1 42 86 01 26 | **Getting there** Métro to Étienne Marcel (Line 4); bus 29 or 39 | **Hours** Mon–Sat 11am–11pm | **Tip** A bit further along, at 60 Rue Réaumur, you can find the Musée des Arts et Métiers, dedicated to science and technology, where you can see Foucault's Pendulum and the calculating machines of Blaise Pascal.

48 La Graineterie du Marché

A unique jumble of seeds to eat and seeds to grow

Behind the picturesque entrance stacked with potted herbs and aromatic plants, hides an exceptional grocery and seed supplier. The shop was originally created by Mr and Mrs Lion in the 1930s, but it became a pet shop in 1975 due to competition from supermarkets. José Ferré took it over in 2004 and restored it to its original trade. The place now looks like a film set from the 1950s, full of period bric-a-brac and hung with old photographs though, on close inspection, many of these are from a later era – José is an admirer of the Rolling Stones.

In the first room, everything is edible. You will find packets of all types of flours (wheat, chestnut, chickpea and rice), pots of jams, honeys, mustards and mayonnaise, tins of sardines, tuna and fish soup, all from La Belle-Iloise, bottled oils, vinegars and sauces, various types of rice and pasta, pulses and dry lentils. But he also sells a great variety of produce *en vrac* (in tubs to help yourself, each marked with a colourful painted plate), such as organic flours, couscous and maize, semolina, lentils, soya beans and haricots géants, chickpeas, bulgur wheat, quinoa, barley, a bewildering variety of rice, dried fruits, nuts, kasha, teas and infusions, and dozens of spices.

The sweets are a memory lane for French children: the Véritable Gaufrette Amusante (biscuits with a little message stamped across them), the Anis de Flavigny, little sweet aniseed balls, pain d'épices, delicious spicy gingerbread from Mulot & Petitjean (the oldest pain d'épices factory in Dijon) and the Bêtises de Cambrai (traditional boiled sweets).

The back room is the garden shop, packed with seeds, fertilisers, pesticides (many natural), tools and bird food. And littered among all these is a kind of flea market selling old-fashioned tables and knick-knacks of the 1940s and 50s. Few leave without clutching something.

Address 8 Place d'Aligre, 75012 Paris, +33 (0)1 43 43 22 64 | **Getting there** Métro to Faidherbe-Chaligny (Line 8); bus 57 or 86 | **Hours** Tue–Sat 9am–1pm & 4–7.30pm, Sun 9am–1pm | **Tip** At 199 Rue de Charenton there is a beautiful building dating back to 1911. Its façade is remarkable for the two windows on the first floor framed with Atlas figures representing a miner, a peasant, a worker and a sailor.

49 La Grande Épicerie du Bon Marché

The most luxurious spread

A section of one of Paris' most elegant department stores is dedicated to food. At its heart is La Place du Marché – the market place, where you can find only the best fruit, vegetables and herbs. Ranged round this centre are the specialities, all clearly labelled. La Poissonerie sells only the freshest day's catch. La Boucherie sells matured meats, displayed inside a fridge with glass windows, their *cave de maturation*, where exceptional cuts of meat are aged and hung before the customers' eyes. Nearby, La Rôtisserie and La Charcuterie smell deliciously of roasted chicken, saucisson sec (salamis of various types) and meat pies. At La Fromagerie there is a selection of more than 120 carefully chosen cheeses. At La Pâtisserie, you can indulge in a Saint-Honoré (which has to be eaten the day the special crème is made) or a charlotte Mont-Blanc. At La Boulangerie, let yourself be tempted by a warm baguette. At La Cuisine, you can choose a salad or a cooked meal to take away. Le Luxe counter offers caviar, truffles and smoked salmon. Basic products, from Scottish oats to Italian tinned tomatoes, are ranged along the shelves in between, including teas, coffees, juices, beers and cordials, and downstairs there's a beautiful cellar selling more than 3,000 different wines. And between all these counters there are high tables where you can sit and sip a glass of wine, and take a light bite, of oysters, perhaps, at La Poissonnerie. There is really no reason to go anywhere else, if you have the money. Ironically, *bon marché* means 'cheap' in French – which is exactly what Bon Marché isn't.

The shop has quite a story. In 1852, Aristide Boucicaut and his wife Marguerite created the first modern department store, where you could enter freely and walk among the counters without being bothered, but definitely tempted. This new concept in retail became a model for the world.

Address 38 Rue de Sèvres, 75007 Paris, +33 (0)1 44 39 81 00 | Getting there Métro to Sèvres-Babylone (Line 10 or 12); bus 68, 83 or 94 | Hours Mon–Sat 8.30am–9pm, Sun 10am–8pm | Tip La Fondation EDF, at 6 Rue Récamier, often shows excellent exhibitions, based on new technologies. It's a good idea to check their programme on the internet. At the time of writing, it was showing video games through the years.

50 La Grande Mosquée

A haven of peace, with lots to eat

Walking through the gateway to the restaurant of La Grande Mosquée is like being transported from the busy street into another world of quietude and peace. You step immediately into a garden, which is shaded by trees and delightful at any time of year, but especially beautiful and cool in the height of summer. It's tempting to take a pastry from the display in an inner doorway, sit down at once at one of the many tables and sip a cup of mint tea. But if you go further, new delights await you – a progression of high inner rooms, richly decorated in Moorish style with intricate patterned tiling and hung with exotic lamps. There are arched verandas all around, providing comfortable, cosy corners for quiet conversations.

The food is equally rich and exotic. You could start with a brick (a filo pastry envelope stuffed with fried shrimps, tuna or egg), an aubergine salad or an egg chakchouka (a kind of spicy onion, tomato and pepper ratatouille topped with poached eggs), a harira, a Moroccan soup made with chickpeas, spices and herbs, a pastilla (shredded chicken with egg, onion, spices and parsley in a flaky pastry envelope). Then indulge in the main dishes, couscous with lamb or chicken or keftas (minced meat balls) or merguez (lamb sausage). Or go for the royal, with all combined. You can have a lamb tajine, with prunes, almonds and onions, or lamb served with peppers, tomatoes, onions and cinnamon semolina, or a chicken dish served with olives and preserved lemon. Among the grilled meat, you have the choice between keftas or lamb skewers, lamb chops or merguez.

And for dessert? – ice cream, oriental pâtisserie, the Schéhérazade cup (a concoction of strawberry sorbet, coconut, almond milk and fruit salad) or the Oriental (mint-tea sorbet, with pine nuts, honey and ice cream). And what to drink? Water, sodas, fruit juices or mint tea.

Address 39 Rue Geoffroy Saint-Hilaire, 75005 Paris, +33 (0)1 43 31 38 20 | **Getting there** Métro to Censier-Daubenton (Line 7); bus 67 or 91 | **Hours** Salon de Thé daily 9am–midnight; restaurant midday and evening | **Tip** The Muséum National d'Histoire Naturelle, with its Grand Gallery of Evolution, full of amazing specimens of animals and insects, is just across the street.

51__Gravity Bar
Taste on the piste

Marc Longo is a fan of *sports de glisse*. This French term covers both surfing and skiing – basically, sports that slide. This is the theme of Gravity Bar, which Marc and a few friends opened in 2015. Everything in it slides easily down… the throat. Under a ceiling of plywood waves, around a bar that serpentines, you can sip specially concocted cocktails, which, in keeping with the theme, are named according to the nature of the slope: Désorientation, Apesanteur (floating), Exaltation and Sueurs Froides (cold sweats). The wall behind the bar is packed with unusual alcohols and liqueurs (unknown even to me) and rows of herb and fruit syrups almost all of which are homemade. They also stock very good beers, one of which, a white beer called Perle, is truly excellent, and two artisan beers from the Parisian region itself.

The kitchen, which is on view to the customers, is the domain of the young Taiwanese chef, Isabella Lin. The menu, which changes every day, mixes French and Asian cuisine in a very creative way. To give a few examples: hummus of Japanese yuzu miso; ancient varieties of tomatoes, edamame (green soya beans) and slow cooked young onions; home-made terrine – made from free-range guinea fowl, pork and duck liver, apricot and pistachios in cognac; line-caught tuna tartare with baby beetroots (red, yellow and white), blackcurrants, fresh green seaweed and golden sesame seasoning; peppers stuffed with beef and baby shallots, Taiwanese sauce, home-made ricotta, cashew nuts and Thai basil. For dessert, she offers a white nectarine and chocolate fudge; Brittany shortbread and a yoghurt mousse; soft-centred chocolate brownies, cherries and piment d'Espelette.

The plates are served individually or to be shared, and to accompany them they offer a choice selection of natural wines. The terrace is very comfortable with couches in the form of wave designs, of course.

Address 44 Rue des Vinaigriers, 75010 Paris, +33 (0)6 98 54 92 49 | **Getting there** Métro to Jacques Bonsergent (Line 5); bus 56 or 65 | **Hours** Tue–Sat 6pm–2am, dinner 7pm–midnight | **Tip** The Rue des Vinaigriers, though very short, is packed with interesting artisan and design boutiques. It also leads to the very attractive Quai de Valmy, which runs beside the Canal Saint-Martin.

52__Grillé

A kebab unlike any other

Grillé is a little corner shop decorated in blue-and-white tiles, designed by Clément Blanchet, a student of the famous Dutch architect Rem Koolhaas. It contains only a roasting spit, a deep frying pan, an oven and a counter. You couldn't make it simpler. You eat standing or on the sparse supply of stools, inside or out. Everything is focused on the food, which is delicious.

Kebab means any grilled meat in Arabic, but here it's veal specially chosen by Hugo Desnoyer, one of the star butchers in the capital (see ch. 35). The home-made flat Kurdish bread is cooked on the spot from organic flour and petit épeautre (einkorn wheat) from the Moulin des Moines, to a recipe by Jean-Luc Poujauran. You have a choice between four sauces: white (fromage blanc and horseradish), green (green tomato flesh, green pimento and sweet onions), green peas (green peas, cumin, mint and lemon) or tahini (aubergine, fromage blanc and tahini). All of this rolled with salad and fresh herbs. Plus, you get a small or big side order of home-made French fries.

For dessert they offer the excellent ice creams made by Emmanuel Ryon (flavoured according to the mood of the ice cream maker). To drink, there's water, sodas, craft lemonades and beers, Sassy cider and fruit juices by Patrick Font (try the wild peach or Israeli grapefruit). You make the coffee yourself with a choice between Grillé Black (from Peru, Honduras, Sumatra and India), Grillé Origin (Honduras) and Grillé Blend (Peru, Honduras and Éthiopia), all from the Esperanza company.

The only problem is that the place can get very crowded at lunchtime, and long queues can build up, even though the staff are super efficient. Grillé is the creation of Marie Carcassonne, Fréderic Peneau and Hugo Desnoyer, all more used to fine dining than street food, but it's a great success. You can also find them at the Jardin Suspendu (see ch. 60).

Address 15 Rue St Augustin, 75002 Paris, +33 (0)1 42 96 10 64 | **Getting there** Métro to Bourse, Quatre-Septembre (Line 3); bus 20, 29 or 39 | **Hours** Mon & Tue noon–4pm, Wed–Fri noon–9pm, Sat noon–6pm | **Tip** Enjoy your kebab in the Square Louvois with its fountain, which is an homage to the four great rivers of France: the Seine, the Loire, the Garonne and the Saône (and spot the unintentional mistake – the last should be the Rhone!).

53__Ground Control
A collective enterprise of excellence

Ground Control has taken over a former SNCF distribution centre, a site stretching over 6,000 square metres. In the cavernous hall, the choice of eating is enormous. Several famous restaurants have taken stalls there – and they're worth going for alone. Mr Zhao offers its re-invented traditional Chinese cuisine (main address 37 Rue des Jeûneurs 75002); at Faggio you can taste some of the best pizzas in Paris (main address 72–74 Rue de Rochechouart 75009); Chilam presents its brilliant 100 per cent home-made Mexican food (main address 12 Rue des Écouffes 75004). And there are many discoveries to be made: at Solina you'll find fresh pasta made in the purest Abruzzo tradition; La Résidence invites talented refugee chefs to show their skills under the auspices of the Refugees Food Festival (when I was there Magda Gegenava, the famous Georgian chef, was at the oven); L'Estaminet offers a choice of coffees, chocolates, fresh fruit juice plus a brunch; at Table Nali, it's African fusion and women's recipes; Le Décanteur is a sympathetic wine bar with a very select menu that changes all the time; Douglas offers sodas, organic fruit or vegetable juices, teas, wines, beers, spirits, cocktails and aperitifs.

All this in a cheerful atmosphere around big wooden tables and 100 per cent recycled furniture, which humanise the huge hall. Outside there is an extensive container garden where you can choose between many street foods: burgers and fish and chips; focaccias and fresh salads; pitta sandwiches, falafels; pancakes and crêpes; winkles, accras (fried fish balls) and crayfish meat salad.

The Ferme de Gally created the urban vegetable garden where you can rest on deck chairs, read or work in the shade of the many olive trees. Ground Control also organises a huge array of activities, from tarot card readings to sophrology (a form of dynamic relaxation) and ceramic painting.

Address 81 Rue du Charolais, 75012 Paris | **Getting there** Métro to Gare de Lyon (Line 1); bus 29 | **Hours** Wed–Fri midday–midnight, Sat 11am –midnight, Sun 11am–10.30pm | **Tip** On Avenue Daumesnil you can climb up to the Coulée Verte, a beautiful garden installed along a disused raised railway line between Bastille and the Porte de Vincennes, another example of the 'greening' of Paris.

54_La Guinguette d'Angèle

'Here are fruits, flowers, leaves and branches…

…And here is my heart which beats only for you.' It's difficult not to think of the famous poem by Verlaine when you chance upon La Guinguette d'Angèle. *Guinguette* has no equivalent in English (largely due to the weather) – it's an unpretentious, open-air café where people can drink and dance. Angèle's guinguette is totally unpretentious and delightful, but, it has to be said, there's not much room for dancing, or even sitting.

The takeaway menu, which is vegan and gluten-free, changes every day. On the day we visited, on offer were Thai and red rice, with tamari and savory, smoked tofu with sesame, rocket hummus and almond purée, and roasted celeriac with vanilla. The hot dish was Gorgonzola creamed vegetables with quinoa. For dessert, there were cookies and brownies, little tarts, chia seed pudding, with almond sauce, coconut yoghurt and fresh fruit. But you can also find energy balls (made of nuts and raisins), and acai bowls (made from the very trendy, dried palm-tree berry that comes from Amazonia), along with detox drinks with apple, pineapple, banana, cucumber, orange and verbena (in case you'd spent all night in a real guinguette).

Angèle Ferreux-Maeght springs from a family of famous art collectors in France. She grew up between the family farm, near Grasse, and Paris. After working at the famous Ferry Building Organic Market in San Francisco, and then in Australia, she met Céleste Candido who introduced her to naturopathic medicine. She founded a catering service based on these ideas, which enjoyed success in the fashion world. La Guingette d'Angèle is only one string to her bow: she has a cosy and relaxed restaurant in the Rue du General Renault, another at the Hotel Bonpoint where you can eat in the charming Jardin à la Francaise, and every Sunday at midday Angèle offers a vegan and organic brunch at the Alcazar restaurant.

Address 34 Rue Coquillère, 75001 Paris, +33 (0)9 80 61 25 49 | **Getting there** Métro to Les Halles (Line 4); bus 67, 74, 85 | **Hours** Mon–Fri 11.30am–3pm | **Tip** The very elegant and chic Galerie Véro-Dodat, 19 Rue Jean-Jacques Rousseau, is the only covered arcade in this quartier. Even though very short, it gives an illusion of depth thanks to the diamond-shaped black-and-white marble tiles on the floor.

55 __ Gyoza Bar

A Japanese take on Chinese ravioli

The gyoza is a stuffed, horn-shaped ravioli. It's of Chinese origin, dating back 1,500 years. It was traditionally eaten at New Year, which might explain the new moon shape. Guillaume Guedj had the bright idea, with a Japanese chef, to reinvent these special raviolis using only the finest ingredients. The fillings (made from meat from Hugo Desnoyer's butchery) and the pasta (made with tender wheat flour) are prepared in the kitchen above the bar. But the gyozas themselves are cooked in the smallest of kitchens before your eyes.

In a minimalist setting – the walls are lined with stones – you can eat at the counter or at one of the few tables in front or in the passage outside. The cook works with four small ovens that look like flat, deep waffle moulds into which she first pours a little layer of oil. She puts the raviolis into this, closes the lid, and then at the moment she judges right, opens it to drizzle on more hot oil. Then she shuts it again. You can sense her personal involvement in getting the timing exactly right for your dish.

You have a choice of eight or twelve pieces according to your appetite. The stuffing is delicately seasoned, smooth and moist, made with minced pork, chicken, prawns or beef, and there is always a vegetarian option. The gyozas arrived with a citrus-flavoured soy sauce.

Side dishes include marinated soya sprouts, Japanese green peas, white rice or a nitamago. This is a cold, soft-boiled egg, which has been marinated before cooking for 24 hours in a mix of soy sauce, sake, rice vinegar, miso, sugar and ginger – unfamiliar, but enjoyable, even if you don't like eggs very much. Red or white wine is served by the glass, as well as a white beer with yuzu, a citrus with a lemon taste, or a red beer with sansho, a Japanese pepper with a citrus flavour, and various teas. The bar offers takeaway until 2.30pm.

Address 56 Passage des Panoramas, 75002 Paris, +33 (0)1 44 82 00 62 | **Getting there**
Métro to Grands Boulevards (Line 8 or 9); bus 67 or 74 | **Hours** Mon–Sat noon–2pm &
6.30–11.30pm | **Tip** In the passage there are also two excellent restaurants, Passage 53
(chic and top class) and Racines, a casual Italian bistro with creative cooking and serving
natural wines.

56__Holybelly 5
Paris learns from the world

Sarah Mouchot and Nico Alary opened Holybelly in 2013 with the credo 'good food, good coffee, good service'. Originally from Beauvais, they worked in Vancouver and Melbourne. Impressed by the cafés and restaurants they found there, they had the brave idea of importing the concept of the modern, international coffee shop back to its original source, in Paris. The atmosphere is relaxed, the staff friendly and super efficient. As for the coffee: it comes from the Brûlerie de Belleville and is served as espresso, allongé, filtre, au lait, crème and noisette. Or you can have a slightly spiced hot chocolate or choose one of the many teas. If you're lactose intolerant, ask for oat milk.

Their brunch has acquired mythical status, served every day from 9am to 4pm. There are six different savoury, sweet, vegan and gluten-free options, served with home-made pancakes, home-made granola, pain des amis (bread that comes straight from the oven of Christophe Vasseur (see ch. 36), with butter and home-made jam.

Their set menu raises a smile for its unorthodox richness: you choose between poached, fried or scrambled eggs, which come with smoky bacon marinated in maple syrup, hash browns, fried mushrooms with thyme and garlic, a pork and fennel galette, marinated feta or a young shoots salad. There are two fresh dishes of the day. I ordered the hot dog, Holybelly style (home-made brioche bread, Montbéliard sausage, a seasoning with gherkins, fried onions, sweet potato fries and herb yoghurt sauce). I still salivate at the memory of it! They have also the Super Cheesy Quesadilla (a wheat tortilla garnished with cheese, piquillos, fried mushrooms, chimichurri sauce and pimento cream). The puddings change every day as well – when I visited there was a choice of chocolate and courgette cake or an ultra-light cheesecake. To drink: fruit juice, lemonade, iced tea, Deck & Donohue beer, cider and cocktails.

Address 5 Rue Lucien Sampaix, 75010 Paris, +33 (0)1 82 28 00 80 | **Getting there** Métro to Jacques Bonsergent (Line 5); bus 56 or 65 | **Hours** Daily 9am–4pm | **Tip** At no. 35 you can see a building in the Art Nouveau style, handsomely decorated with brightly coloured ceramic tiles.

57 _ I Golosi
The flowering of an Italian passion

Marc Tonozzo, the boss of I Golosi, is a larger-than-life Venetian, a standard-bearer of Italian food in France. The walls are hung with the diplomas he's received, such as the Grand Prix de la Presse du Vin in 2005, the Gambero Rosso in 2012 and the diploma of the Unione Regionale Cuochi Toscani. Marc Tonazzo has been running his shop-cum-restaurant for 25 years, and every aspect of I Golosi (in English it means 'the greedy ones') is imbued with his personality. It's worth a visit just to meet him.

I Golosi serves only seasonal vegetables and its menu changes every week. It cleverly combines classic dishes with Tonozzo's lively imagination. When I visited, the menu offered as an antipasto: mozzarella and courgette rissoles on a basil and tomato coulis; a young cabbage salad with Rainier cherries (a fine yellow orange variety), grapes and pine nuts; a rocket salad with olives from the Marches, dried tomatoes and smoked duck breast; a panzanella Toscana (a salad of vegetables and bread, lightly soaked in olive oil and vinegar and flavoured with basil), which I loved. As a starter, they offer a Trento speck (smoked pork fillet) risotto with Parmesan; a pasta dish with fresh peas and roasted belly of pork; and Spaghetti alla Puttanesca (sautéed with tomatoes, anchovies and capers).

The main dishes were: poached ray wing, flavoured with lemon and a salad; veal cooked slowly in tarragon with new potatoes from Puglia; linguini with blue lobster, delicately flavoured with pimento and basil. Only the classic Italian desserts don't change: tiramisu and a panna cotta made without gelatine. And, of course, a board of the finest Italian cheeses.

The shop is superbly stocked, with about 500 different Italian wines, the famous pastas of Martelli and Monograno Felicetti and many other delicacies. The best of Italy is tucked into a little street in the heart of Paris.

Address 6 Rue de la Grange Batelière, 75009 Paris, +33 (0)1 48 24 18 63 | **Getting there** Métro to Grands Boulevards (Line 8 or 9); bus 20, 39, 48, 67 or 74 | **Hours** Mon–Fri noon–2.30pm & 7.30–10.30pm, Sat noon–2.30pm | **Tip** The restaurant gives onto the Passage Verdeau which is well known for its shops selling vintage postcards and old illustrated books.

58 Ibrik Coffee Shop

An Eastern European concoction of good eating

Ibrik is a one-off, a personal search for identity through food. Cathy, the owner, has a complex background. Her father is a Romanian artist, her mother Greek, but she was brought up largely in France, where she began her career in finance. But she wanted to find a more personal form of expression and came up with the happy, if slightly bizarre, idea to open an eatery that combined Balkan with Byzantine cooking in Paris. It works a treat.

You start with mezze: hummus, aubergine caviar, vegetarian keftas with garlic sauce. To follow: dakos – feta cheese with chopped tomatoes, olives and lemon seasoning; keftas made with white bean hummus, pickles and slow-cooked onion; roasted and marinated tzatziki chicken; Greek salad – feta cheese with tomatoes, cucumber and Kalamata olives; Ibrik salad with Mizithra – goat's cheese – with spelt, roasted pumpkin, spinach shoots and basil; a vegetarian or meat pitta, the latter made with roast chicken, red onions and lemon mayonnaise. Among the pâtisseries is a delicious, soft pistachio cake with a lemon and rose glaze, and other desserts based on Greek yoghurt. Ibrik also serves nourishing, meal-in-one bowls: Le Greek (containing yoghurt, home-made granola, seasonal fruit, dates, figs and pistachios) and Le Bircher (containing muesli, farm milk, yoghurt, fresh seasonal fruit, hazelnuts, almonds and honey). Their oil, cheeses and olives come from Profil Grec (see ch. 93).

To drink, there's freshly squeezed lemon juice, teas, infusions, hot chocolate and the unbelievable Ibrik, which has given its name to the place. This is made in the Hovoli – a magnificent, eagle-topped, brass coffee-making machine, which stands proudly in the middle of the shop. It makes a delicious Turkish-type coffee with precisely measured, freshly ground beans, brewed on a bed of sand. In November 2018 they opened a restaurant, Ibrik 2:2, at 9 Rue de Mulhouse 75002.

Address 43 Rue Laffitte, 75009 Paris, +33 (0)1 73 71 84 60 | **Getting there** Métro to Notre-Dame-de-Lorette (Line 12); bus 42 | **Hours** Mon–Fri 8.30am–4.30pm, Sat 11.30am–5.30pm | **Tip** This street is famous in the history of art. One of France's greatest art dealers, Ambroise Vollard, had his galleries at nos. 6 and 37, where he sold paintings from Cézanne to Picasso. Claude Monet was born at no. 45 in 1840.

59 __ Izraël
The paradise of spices

Izraël is a fantastic Aladdin's cave of spices from around the world. As soon as you cross its threshold you are hit by a feast of smells and colours. The shelves, which go from floor to ceiling, are stacked with jams and marmalades of every kind, seasonings, oils and vinegars, Italian, Greek and Spanish olives, jars of marinated peppers and pimentos, bottles of liqueurs and spirits, cases full of vanilla pods (often of rare varieties according to availability), stacks of 'touron' (a type of Spanish nougat), Turkish Delight and a variety of confectionery from many countries.

The floor is packed with bags, baskets and bins full of various spices, peppers from Timut, Malabar and Pondicherry, paprika, sumac, pimento from Espelette, Colombo curry, nutmeg and mace, ras-el-hanout (the spice mix used in Morocco), and a whole variety of blends, many made by hand by Françoise, the owner. Here you will find cereals and pulses, such as chickpeas, rice, lentils and beans (broad, coco and borlotti), dried nuts – walnuts, hazelnuts and peanuts – and dried raisins and berries.

It would be almost impossible to enumerate all of them, for hardly a centimetre of the shop is left free, so much so that there's barely room for customers! If you have come across a rare spice on holiday in Turkmenistan or China, the chances are that you will find it at Izraël. As if the shop didn't have enough, it's also a prime supplier of fresh Corsican and Oriental charcuterie. The shop has become a favourite of the famous Cuban novelist and poet, Zoé Valdés, who lives in Paris.

If it's good, you will find it here – this is the owners' motto. Fortunately, they know where everything is, and can find anything. The only slight drawback is that the strain of doing so can tell a little. But whether you enter at random, or in search of something rare, few customers ever leave empty handed.

Address 30 Rue François Miron, 75004 Paris, +33 (0)1 42 72 66 23 | **Getting there** Métro to Saint-Paul (Line 1); bus 67, 69, 76 or 96 | **Hours** Tue–Sat 11am–1pm & 2–7pm | **Tip** Almost in front of it, at nos. 11–13, there are two medieval half-timbered houses restored during the 1970s. At 7–5 Rue de Fourcy there is the Maison Européenne de la Photographie.

60__Le Jardin Suspendu

A modern Hanging Gardens of Babylon

This brilliant new initiative is a joint enterprise between Viparis, which organises the city's big trade fairs, and Passage Piéton, which invents participatory experiences for a wide public. In 2018, they transformed the top deck of the the Parc des Expo car park into an exceptional public venue for the whole family, with unbelievable views right across Paris. The vast space has been turned into a garden, with lemon and olive trees and flowers in containers. The company Peas and Love has installed about 20 allotment plots, which people can book at the beginning of the season to grow their own fruit and vegetables. There's one car left, with its bonnet open, and plants growing out of its engine.

The food stalls, which look like garden sheds, offer excellent fare: L'Atelier Fratelli offers their famous focaccias, their tartuffo, with black truffle cream and herb-cooked ham, and their bufala, with pesto, mozzarella, Parmesan and tomatoes. Grillé (see ch. 52) serves delicious kebabs made with suckling veal from Aveyron. Vapeurs offers steamed dumplings, Hong Kong-style. L'Avocatier serves open sandwiches garnished with a range of toppings. L'Apéro Balibert offers dishes based on salami and pâté from the Basque region. La Petite Épicerie sells local products from Balibert. And Häagen-Dazs has made new ice creams especially for the Jardin Suspendu. There are drink stalls everywhere, serving champagnes, beers, wines, cocktails, fruit juices and teas. And there's a gigantic screen, concerts and conferences, yoga and sophrology classes, music and dancing. The venue can be hired for private events on Mondays and Tuesdays and can accommodate 1,000 people.

Le Jardin Suspendu was open from the 14 June to 2 September in 2018. Its location may change, or not, in the future – but its huge success ensures it will happen again – somewhere – so check on the internet.

Address Facing 40 Rue d'Oradour-sur-Glane, 75015 Paris | **Getting there** Métro to Porte de Versailles (Line 12); bus 80; tram T3a | **Hours** Wed 6–11pm, Thu 6pm–midnight, Fri & Sat 6pm–2am, Sun midday–11pm | **Tip** At the Quai de Javel, the Parc André Citroën is a beautiful modern formal French garden created on the site of the previous Citroën factory. It is the creation of two landscape gardeners, Gilles Clément and Allain Provost, and has many remarkable features.

61__Jean-Paul Hévin
From footballs to stiletto heels, all in chocolate

In 1976, Jean-Paul Hévin met Joël Robuchon, one of the most famous Michelin three-star cooks in France, in the Hôtel Nikko in Paris. It was Jean-Paul's first experience of working with an absolute master in his profession, and his meteoric career took off from there. He took the first prize in Pâtisserie in France, but had global ambitions. After years of working in Japan, he returned in triumph to Paris. He is now a Meilleur Ouvrier de France, and widely acknowledged as one of the finest chocolatiers in the world.

Jean-Paul Hévin personally selects his cacao from plantations in Brazil, Ecuador, Peru and Madagascar. It's worth going to his shop for his exquisite individual chocolates and tablets, but he has so much more to offer. He is a superb pâtissier as well as a chocolatier and makes little macarons, croquants (a type of crunchy biscuit), madeleines and florentines, pâtisseries like the vanilla-stawberry or vanilla-blackcurrant vacherins with a base of meringue and Chantilly cream. His Mazaltov is a very light cheese cake, as melt-in-the-mouth as his pear soufflé tartlet. And, of course, he makes a supreme chocolate tart. But my favourite of all is his Mont Blanc – a hazelnut meringue with vanilla Chantilly, topped with chestnut paste threads, which look for the world like wriggling worms – divine!

In keeping with his global ambitions, Jean-Paul Hévin makes a cake called Rio topped with a figure of Jesus Christ and a football, a JFK decorated with a Statue of Liberty and an apple, and a Moscow emblazoned with a hammer and sickle and a model of the Kremlin. If you want a present from Paris you can choose an Eiffel Tower, a lady's stiletto shoe, or a lace heart – all made in chocolate of course. These can be sent to anywhere in the world. Jean-Paul Hévin now has several boutiques in Paris and shops in Tokyo, Hiroshima, Hong Kong and Taiwan.

Address 3 Rue Vavin, 75006 Paris, +33 (0)1 43 54 09 85 | **Getting there** Métro to Vavin (Line 4); bus 58 or 82 | **Hours** Tue–Sat 10.30am–7.30pm | **Tip** At 100 bis Rue d'Assas is the Musée Zadkine, where the Russian sculptor had his workshop, and a delightful garden.

62 Joséphine Bakery
The delicious taste of fresh baking

Benoît Castel established this little shop in 2012 after a career as Chef Pâtissier at the La Grande Épicerie (see ch. 49). Here everything is made in-house, the breads are kneaded and cooked on the spot and the pastries are kept simple, and with no artificial colouring. And the basic ingredients used are all of the highest quality, not just for the breads and cakes, but also for the sandwiches, salads and quiches. The flour comes from the Moulins Bourgeois, which grinds only organic wheat.

The sandwiches include the classic ham and butter, with or without Emmental cheese, saucisson and butter or rillettes with pickled gherkins. Those with raw vegetables come with ham and Emmental, chicken or goat's cheese. Finally, they offer two specialities: smoked salmon with fromage frais or Brie with walnuts and rocket. The salads are delicious: lentils, peas and lardons; pasta with tomatoes, mozzarella and olives; ham and melon; chicken, olives, Parmesan and lettuce; and a detox with beans, broccoli, broad beans, peas, rocket and coriander.

For dessert, there's fromage blanc with a fruit coulis or fruit salad, and, of course, a range of delicious pâtisseries to choose from: chocolate mousse, cherry clafoutis, raspberry and pistachio tartlets, coffee or chocolate choux buns, raspberry cheesecake, lemon tart, far Breton, brownies, vanilla shortbread in the form of a Petit Lu cake (in honour of Benoît Castel's Breton origins) and, depending on the season, Benoît's signature dish, a fabulous cream tart. Besides all this they offer a traditional baguette, pain du coin, rye bread, pain de mie and pavé tradition together with cakes, viennoiseries, madeleines, financiers, biscuits, and home-made jams. To drink: espresso, a short cream coffee, a longer one with milk, hot chocolate, black or green tea, soda and organic fruit juices. You can sit along the small counter, or take away.

Sandwich classique

- Jambon Emmental Beurre
- Jambon Beurre
- Saucisson Beurre   4 €20
- Rillette Cornichon

Sandwich crudités :

- Jambon Emmental crudités
- Poulet crudités
- Thon crudités   4 €
- Chèvre crudités

Sandwich spécial :

- Saumon fumé fromage frais
- Brie Noix Roquette   6 €

Address 42 Rue Jacob, 75006 Paris, +33 (0)1 42 60 20 39 | **Getting there** Métro to Saint-Germain-des-Prés (Line 4); bus 63 or 86 | **Hours** Mon–Fri 7.30am–8pm | **Tip** At 6 Rue Furstenberg, in the corner of a little square, you can visit the Musée Delacroix, which includes his beautifully-lit studio in a charming private garden.

63 La Laiterie de Paris

Cheese made in Paris

Pierre Coulon began as a farmer in Loire-Atlantique and then spent 15 years working as a cheese maker, before he had the bright idea to bring cheese making back to the capital. He opened La Laiterie de Paris in December 2017 and his rapid success since then has been richly deserved.

His milk comes from specially selected organic farms. He makes and matures his own cheeses, yoghurts and fromage blanc in the back room behind a plate glass window. The small shop in front sells his produce: goat crottins, bûches and pyramides, Saint Félicien cheese, either plain or with honey and hazelnuts, a sheep tomme, his home-made Cheddar and a Sakura (Japanese goat's cheese matured in cherry leaves). The other products come directly from producers he knows, such as: tomme fermière with fennel, Fourme d'Ambert, blue d'Auvergne, Brie Normand bio, Roquefort, Reblochon, Brousse du Larzac, Laguiole d'Aveyron and from Jura Morbier, Comté, Raclette and Cancoillotte (plain or with garlic, shallots or savagnin – a Jura grape). There are several Savoy cheeses, such as Emmental, Abondance, Beaufort and tomme au foin (a cheese matured in dry hay), and a few intriguing rarities like the Manigodine (from the Haute-Savoie), the Artisou (Cantal), the Rigotte de Condrieu and some foreign cheese like Gorgonzola, Stichelton and an organic goat Gouda – all from their country of origin.

The yoghurts, plain or with fruit – some made with goat's milk – are absolutely delicious, all free of artificial colouring and preservatives. They sell a few desserts, such as traditional lemon posset, raw cream and fresh milk and a selection of charcuterie such as ham terrine, rillettes of black pork from Bigorre and delicious syrups made from Menton lemons. Pierre proudly announces on the doorframe that he is the cheese maker who pays the best money to his milk producers. This place deserves everyone's patronage.

Address 74 Rue des Poissonniers, 75018 Paris, contact Facebook @lalaiteriedeparis |
Getting there Métro to Marcadet-Poissonniers (Line 4); bus 60 | **Hours** Tue–Fri 4–8pm,
Sat 10am–8pm | **Tip** When you walk down the Boulevard Barbès you enter into the
Quartier de la Goutte d'Or, a very animated district of Paris with a tremendous mix of
ethnic and exotic produce shops. Don't miss the Marché Dejean on the Rue de Suez.

64__Legrand Filles et Fils
Tasting becomes an institution

La Maison Legrand is not just a place to buy and taste some of the most superb products of France, it's also become a favourite meeting place for politicians, journalists, businessmen and artists. It's a salon in a beautiful 19th-century arcade, and is an exquisite embodiment of luxury.

Fancy buying a Romanée-Conti or a Château Petrus? This is the place where you will find one for sure. Faced with more than 10,000 different wines on offer, from everyday wines to the rarest vintages, champagnes and spirits, the embarrassment of riches makes making choices difficult. At the counter, you can taste a glass of wine with products from the many 'terroirs' of France, prepared raw or cooked. The grocery offers such delicious specialities as olive oil from Nyons, vinegars from Banyuls and Modena, tuna belly, foie gras and sweets from the Coquelicots de Nemours to the Bêtises de Cambrais.

The business began in 1880, when François Beaugé opened a shop in the Rue de la Banque in a previous institution run by the Corporation of Grocers. It had one foot in the establishment from the beginning. It was also immediately a world centre, for customers came there to buy products imported by the Compagnie des Indes from all over the world: spices, teas, coffees, wines and spirits. The two brothers, Pierre and Alexandre Legrand, built on this success. In 1945, Lucien, the eldest son of Pierre, took over. A dynamic, jocund, larger-than-life character, he travelled throughout France to find delicious little-known everyday wines, making La Maison Legrand even more famous. In 1984, his daughter Francine continued the spirit of the establishment, succeeded in 2000 by Gérard Sibourd-Baudry then in 2018, by François Chirumberro. La Maison Legrand organises thematic tastings and visits to vineyards, and on Thursdays, evenings with artists, musicians, writers and poets.

Address 1 Rue de la Banque, 75002 Paris, +33 (0)1 42 60 07 12 | Getting there Métro to Bourse (Line 3); bus 29 | Hours Mon 11am–7pm, Tue–Sat 10am–7.30pm | Tip The Place des Victoires, with its equestrian statue of Louis XIV, is one of the grand royal squares of Paris, along with the Place des Vosges, the Place Vendôme and the Place de la Concorde.

65 __ Levain le Vin
Bread and wine as nature intended

The son of a baker, Christophe Fertillet took the bold step to open this little shop / restaurant in an unlikely corner of Paris in 2016. The French have a phrase *à la fois au four et au moulin*, which means he does everything himself, working at the mill and the oven. Christophe is proud to do it too, because he wants to be open about every aspect of his production. His declared aim is 'to work only with fermented products that are alive, with a guarantee of origin.'

As soon as you enter, you smell the delicious fragrance of fresh bread made with real yeast. All his breads are cooked on the spot with organic flours and yeasts that he has cultivated himself, with sea salts from the Millac salt pans in the Loire-Atlantique. For lunch you can buy sandwiches made with fresh products: the Titi (the familiar name for a young Parisian boy), which is made with traditional bread, Prince de Paris ham, Gruyere cheese, gherkins and slightly salted butter from Beillevaire (see ch. 9); the Extra-muros, made from fig bread, ham, year-aged Comté, olive oil and lemon thyme; the Casse-noisette, made with walnut and raisin bread, Fourme d'Ambert cheese, young salad shoots, walnut oil, cress, garlic and walnuts; the Vegan, made with sesame bread, peppers, tomato, avocado purée, young salad shoots and home-made pickles; the Brutus, made with poppy seed bread, mixed salad, tomato, avocado, olive oil and lemon thyme. The desserts are simple and very good: mini financiers, fromage blanc and chocolate mousse.

In the evening, he offers a Menu Dégustation enabling you to taste the range of his products. There's an Ocean, Earth or Cheese board presented with matching wines and a mixed Yeast Board, offering a selection of his various breads. He serves three beef and three pork charcuteries with two goat's and two cow's cheeses plus an assortment of tapas, which change according to Christophe's lively imagination.

Address 83 Rue du Faubourg Saint-Martin, 75010 Paris, +33 (0)6 61 06 86 13 | **Getting there** Métro to Château d'Eau (Line 4); bus 38 | **Hours** Tue–Sat 11.30am–11pm | **Tip** Next door, at no. 85–87, a plaque reminds you that under the Vichy regime, this former furniture shop was used as a collecting point for the Jews before they were sent to the Drancy internment camp.

66 __ Little India

Indian perfume in the heart of Paris

Tourists wandering into the area between the Gare du Nord and the Métro La Chapelle, suddenly find themselves in Delhi or Jaffna in Sri Lanka. Restaurants invite you in at every step. Treat yourself to a thali – an assortment of dishes on a platter, along with a masala dosa, a crêpe stuffed with spiced curry and vegetables. Don't resist the temptation to wander into VS Co Cash & Carry. This is the temple of all the spices, sauces, chutneys, fruit and vegetables you need to prepare an Indian feast, at unbeatable prices. Alongside the food shops and restaurants you'll find hairdressers, barbers, florists, video rental places (if you fancy a Bollywood night in your room), and shops selling saris, and jewellery to match their brilliant colours.

A bit further south, between the Boulevard de Strasbourg and the Rue du Faubourg St Denis you'll find the Passage Brady – an elegant arcade, built in 1828, and one of the longest in Paris. Its glass roof keeps in all the smells and perfumes of India rising from the spice shops and restaurants along its length.

This is the home of the famous Indian grocery store, Velan, established in 1972 by Antoine Ponnussamy, born in Pondicherry. It's a real treasure trove, full of everything, not just food – kitsch souvenirs, Indian craftwork, jewellery, fabrics, beauty products and every spice you can imagine alongside the papadums, pancakes, pickles, pulses, cereals, dried and glacé fruits, and innumerable nuts of bewildering, unfamiliar varieties.

And here you'll find the many oils and spices used in Ayurvedic medicine, which dates back at least two millennia, and is probably twice as old. The whole principle of this medicine is to bring balance to your system by *not* suppressing natural desires. If this approach to life appeals to you, a visit to Little India, and to the Passage Brady in particular is the best way to start!

Address Rue du Faubourg St Denis, 75010 Paris and Passage Brady, 75010 Paris |
Getting there Métro to Gare du Nord or Château d'Eau (Line 4), La Chapelle (Line 2);
bus 38, 39, 42 or 47 | **Hours** Daily 9.30am–11.30pm | **Tip** At 12 Rue du Faubourg
Saint-Denis have a look at the Passage du Prado, named, oddly, after the Prado Museum
in Madrid, a rare Art Deco survival. In the beginning, it was dedicated to hat-making,
but now it only houses confectioners, repairers, beauty salons, tea rooms and kebab shops.

67 __ Maison Plisson

The total food experience for chic young Parisians

Delphine and Philippe Plisson travelled all over France to choose the produce for their food shop, wine cellar and restaurant, which opened in May 2015. Every product is selected after a 'blind tasting' with strict criteria: each is marked for appearance, texture, smell, taste, and the length of time the taste lingers in the mouth. Any item that scores fewer than 14 points is not selected. 'Naturalness' is a key requirement. Lists of ingredients are combed minutely for the slightest trace of artificial additives. Seasonality is another criterion, for the butchery, charcuterie, cheese counter, creamery, bakery, vegetables and fruit and delicatessen. Waste and transport are reduced to a minimum, since the food in the restaurant is supplied from the shop.

This attention to ecological detail doesn't come cheap, but there is nothing exclusive about this operation. Delphine likes to characterise her restaurant as having an 'at-home' atmosphere. Families with young children are welcomed, with high chairs for babies. There are 120 seats (half on the terrace) arranged in all configurations, including tables d'hôtes for big parties. She even caters for clients in a hurry with high stools at the bar. The menu, from breakfast to mid-evening, is available to take away, and includes salads, meat and fish dishes that change often. On Sunday, there's no brunch but instead a traditional family roast. The ambiance is stylish yet relaxed and the place is always packed.

Their success is due essentially to their quality control, but also to the fact that the cooking in the restaurant earned the blessing of Yves Camdeborde and Bruno Doucet, two of the most famous avant-garde chefs in France. Delphine and Philippe also had the foresight to open their new enterprise in the 3rd Arrondissement – an area that has few food shops but is full of young couples setting up home.

Address 93 Boulevard Beaumarchais, 75003 Paris, +33 (0)1 71 18 19 09 | Getting there Métro to Chemin Vert or Saint-Sébastien–Froissart (Line 8); bus 20, 29, 65 or 96 | Hours Mon 9.30am–9pm, Tue–Sat 8.30am–9pm, Sun 9.30am–8pm | Tip The very trendy shop Merci, at 111 Boulevard Beaumarchais, sells clothes, furnishings, kitchenware – all very chic, in a beautiful environment.

68 Maison Vérot

The finest arts of preparing meat

Here you will find the best jambon persillé, a ham and chopped parsley jelly, a famous Parisian delicacy, alongside the most traditional terrines from the countryside, made from rabbit, pork and veal or lamb sweetbreads, as well as andouillettes and andouilles, types of sausage made from guts and offal – not for the faint-hearted! Not forgetting saucissons, the very different French versions of Italian salami, and of course sausages themselves (there are hundreds of types from all over France), black pudding, pâtés en croûte (cold and sliced meat pies), rillettes (preserved meats), foie gras, prepared meat and vegetable dishes, and delicate puff-pastry crusts, sold filled or empty – everything makes your mouth water at the counter of Maison Vérot.

Jean Vérot opened his charcuterie in 1930 in Saint-Etienne, in the centre of France, and it rapidly became famous across the whole country. His sons Pierre and Alexandre then took over the business, and in 1976 Pierre was nominated 'Meilleur Ouvrier de France'. His son Gilles, with his wife Catherine opened their shop in Paris in 1997. Their credo was to be scrupulously ecological. They have worked with small-scale farmers over many years, and remain firmly rooted in the soil, using meat from animals raised on pesticide-free pastures and only absolutely pure water. Their commitment to traditional recipes has led them to celebrate the extraordinary diversity of the French countryside with its many 'terroirs', producing distinct flavours of meats and vegetables.

In 2008, Gilles and the multi-starred Franco-American chef Daniel Boulud created the Bar Boulud on Broadway, which serves the Maison Vérot's charcuterie with the best French wines. They now have bars in London, Toronto and Boston and Gilles has invented sausages inspired by cooking all over the globe. Charcuterie is about to take over the world!

FROMAGE DE TETE
CHAMPION DE FRANC
1997
le kilo 29,70€

Address 3 Rue Notre-Dame-des-Champs, 75006 Paris, +33 (0)1 45 48 83 32. Also at 7 Rue Lecourbe, 75015 Paris, +33 (0)1 47 34 01 03 and at the Galeries Lafayette Haussmann | **Getting there** Métro to Saint Placide (Line 4); bus 68 | **Hours** Tue–Fri 8.30am–8pm, Sat 8.30am–7.30pm | **Tip** At 53 Rue Notre-Dame-des-Champs, the Centre Culturel du Lucernaire always has a lively programme of theatre, cinema and photography exhibitions. They also have a bistro on the site.

69 Le Marché d'Aligre

A village in Paris

The Aligre market, popular and trendy at the same time, is composed of two parts: the covered market inside, called the Halle Beauvau, and the uncovered market along the Rue d'Aligre. It is one of the oldest markets in Paris, after Le Marché des Enfants Rouges, in the 3rd Arrondissment (see ch. 70).

The interior is a huddle of closely packed stalls of fishmongers, butchers, delicatessens, cheesemongers and bakers. At the Marée Beauvau you will only find fish of supreme freshness, sardine turnovers with piment d'Espelette, smoked red tuna, smoked tuna with sesame seeds, tuna chorizo, avocado and crab salad and octopus salad. At the Boucherie Hayée you will find carpaccio, skewers of lamb, Spanish salami and hams, home-made sausages and merguez and, every day, suckling pig on the spit. There is another very big stall specialising in Italian produce next to another selling cheese from all over France and abroad. At the Volailles d'Aligre, you will find all sorts of poultry and game. The Maison Brard stocks a great variety of regional products. Jojo & Co tempts you with the superb and refined pâtisseries of Johanna Roques (made from organic eggs, AOC butter and fruit fresh from the market). At the Comptoir des Fromages et de la Bière, you can taste one of several dozen beers while nibbling some olives, cheese or tapenade on a slice of bread. The Babbaluscio de Miss Lunch invites you to a meal made entirely of vegetables, both for the main course and the dessert. She offers soups, salads, stuffed vegetables, cakes and ice creams. She also sells books, ceramics, tea towels and some products from the island of Pantelleria.

There are many more fruit and vegetable stalls along the street outside, some selling organic and exotic produce, and others in the main square selling second-hand goods, clothes and antiques – all adding to the jolly hubbub.

Address Place and Rue d'Aligre, 75012 Paris | **Getting there** Métro to Ledru-Rollin (Line 8); bus 57 or 86 | **Hours** Tue – Sat 8am – 1.30pm & 4 – 7.30pm, Sun 8am – 1.30pm | **Tip** Along the Rue du Faubourg Saint-Antoine (mainly on the odd numbers side) there are a number of alleys and passageways that are vestiges of a time when the area was mainly the home of artisans.

70 __ Le Marché des Enfants Rouges

The oldest covered market in Paris

A gateway at the side of the narrow Rue de Bretagne leads to an open square that's almost completely filled with a charming old covered market. The flow of fresh air, glimpses of sky and smells of fresh produce make you feel that you've been transported to a village, and are no longer in the heart of Paris. This market is in fact the oldest in the city, established in 1628. It was named after the children from the nearby orphanage, who always wore red, the colour of Christian charity. There are fruit and vegetable stalls of every kind, and others selling cheeses and fish, alongside grocers and florists. You can shop in peace, taking your time to select what's on offer. But what makes the place especially magical is the number of places where you can eat.

What's remarkable is the quality of what's on offer, at reasonable prices in a most relaxed atmosphere. BiBoViNo, famous for its high-quality natural wines from all over France, has a terrace here. Les Enfants du Marché offers real gastronomic cooking – I had whelks in a marinated sauce with thyme and bay leaves, made by Chef Masahide Ikuta. Le Burger Fermier, with its home-made French fries, is delicious. And Chez Taeko is arguably one of the best and most reasonable Japanese restaurants in Paris.

And then the unforgettable, loquacious Alain Roussel offers what he claims are the best and biggest sandwiches in the world. You have a choice between pastrami, raw ham, cooked jambon, Comté or Salers cheese (he lets you taste some if you can't choose) or smoked trout (the finest in the world according to him – I agree, it's exceptional) – all served with lashings of cooked onions and mushrooms, tomato, avocado and salad, sprinkled with herbs and spices. It's totally crazy: I couldn't finish mine. Success has led him to open another outlet at 26 Rue Charlot – where, hardly surprisingly, there's always a queue.

Address 39–41 Rue de Bretagne, 75003 Paris, +33 (0)1 40 11 20 40 | **Getting there** Métro to Filles du Calvaire (Line 8); bus 20, 29, 75, 96 | **Hours** Tue, Wed, Fri & Sat 8.30am–8.30pm, Thu 8.30am–9.30pm, Sun 8.30am–5pm; restaurants open for dinner | **Tip** At 60 Rue des Francs Bourgeois is the Musée des Archives Nationales in the splendid Hôtel de Soubise, which puts on fascinating exhibitions of its collections.

71 Mariage Frères

The complete tea experience

The French used not to be famous tea-drinkers, but Mariage Frères now offers the widest range of teas anywhere in the world. It lists about 700 varieties from 30 different countries. Alongside the yellow teas from China – among the oldest in the world – the black teas from India and Sri Lanka, green teas from Japan, are exceptions like the oolong blue tea of New Zealand, the caffeine-rich maté from South America and the Scottish white tea, a rarity from Dalreoch. They also sell plant and fruit infusions that are closely related to teas, such as rooibos (redbush), a herbal tea without tannin, from South Africa.

The staff, dressed in linen suits (beige in the shop, white in the tearooms), know everything about what they are selling, for Mariage Frères familiarise themselves closely with the cultivation, harvesting and processing of all the teas they sell, to ensure that only the finest products pass their counters.

Henri and Edouard Mariage established Mariage Frères in 1854, importing quality teas for rich estates, exclusive delicatessen shops, tearooms and the grandest hotels. Some 130 years later they began to open their own retail shops, first in Paris and then abroad. My favourite is one of the oldest in the Rue du Bourg-Tibourg in the Marais, where you can enjoy the complete tea experience: sip a cup in the leafy, light and airy tearoom at the back, visit the charming tea museum upstairs, treat yourself to a teapot in all manner of shapes and colours, from glass to ceramic, cast iron to silver, and of course buy some tea itself, from the row upon row of black storage boxes decorated with the famous yellow label. Teas are classed by colour – black, white, green, yellow and even blue – according to the process of drying, oxidising and sometimes fermentation. But until you go to Mariage Frères, you don't realise that tea has a rainbow of tastes to offer.

Address 30 Rue du Bourg-Tibourg, 75004 Paris, +33 (0)1 42 72 28 11 | **Getting there** Métro to Hôtel de Ville or Saint-Paul (Line 1 or 11); bus 69, 75, 76 or 96 | **Hours** Daily 10.30am–7.30pm (Salon de Thé noon–7pm) | **Tip** Stroll in the Marais area, where there's always a lot going on, and hundreds of trendy little boutiques, bistros and restaurants.

72_Mavrommatis

A unique blend of Greece and France

When Mr Mavrommatis, the founder of this unique shop, came to Paris in 1976 to complete his education, cooking was far from his mind. But, doing little jobs in restaurants, he was, as the French say *'pris au jeu'* – drawn into the game. He decided to open a grocery, with his brother, selling Greek products. Then, realising his ambition was being restricted, he began to create takeaway dishes combining the French techniques he was learning with the local Greek and Cypriot cuisine that he loved. Since 1981, the Mavrommatis brothers (now three of them) have sustained and augmented his original initiative, with growing success.

They developed their exceptional range of dishes using only fresh products, without additives and preservatives. Among the cold starters they offer: ktipiti – whipped feta, Greek yoghurt and pine nuts on a base of grilled peppers; thalassini – a tarama made with organic salmon; smoked aubergine salad with marinated onions, tomatoes, olive oil, lemon and piment d'Espelette; dolmades with organic vine leaves from Chalkidiki stuffed with Arborio rice, dill and pine nuts; olive oil sardine fillets, dried tomatoes and Greek green pimento. Among the warm starters: courgette bricks stuffed with feta, Parmesan and basil; slow-cooked lamb shoulder pastilla, with marinated lemon, honey, dried fruit, parsley and cinnamon; chicken kefta – chicken rissoles stuffed with fresh mushrooms and mixed spices. Among the hot dishes: meat or vegetable stuffed aubergines; lahanodolmades – cabbage leaves stuffed with lamb, Arborio rice, parsley, pine nuts, mint, cumin, cinnamon; lamb and veal or vegetarian moussaka. Their desserts are delicious, such as their pistachio and chocolate cake and their mahalepi – a milk-flavoured orange blossom cream and pistachio. They also offer lunch boxes and cater for events. They now have several other outlets – see the internet.

Address 47 Rue Censier, 75005 Paris, +33 (0)1 45 35 64 95 | **Getting there** Métro to Censier-Daubenton (Line 7); bus 47 | **Hours** Daily 9.30am–9.30pm | **Tip** Visit the Botanical Garden, part of the Jardin des Plantes, where the Alpine Garden displays more than 2,000 species. There are several superb greenhouses, one of which dates back to the 17th century. There are a number of entrances, the nearest of which is in Rue Buffon.

73__MELT
The have-to-go Texan barbecue

Fancy a Texan barbecue in the heart of Paris? MELT transports you to an authentic culinary experience of the Southern United States, with all the warm feeling and smells of a family barbecue. Always working with the best ingredients, the MELT team cooks in a traditional way, with wood (French oak) and great care over many hours until they achieve a perfect balance between smoke, time and taste, in a huge smoke-filled oven that was imported directly from the States. The cooking lasts from four to eighteen hours according to the meat, at low temperatures, and the oven is kept burning 24/7. It's visible just behind the counter. You can't get closer to your food.

On the menu are rib and brisket of beef (American Black Angus), deliciously juicy pork spare-ribs (the Spanish breed Duroc), scrumptiously crisp, or half a chicken (Label Rouge from France), marinated, grilled and coated with a secret sauce. The side dishes are vegetables of the season (fried, marinated, pickled or seasoned), coleslaw and home-made French fries. The puddings are simple but perfect endings to the meal: cookies, brownies or fruit salads. The corn bread is extra.

You order at the counter in the Texan way, and sit down in the room in twos, fours or as a crowd in a totally relaxed atmosphere. For drinks, there's a choice between a few natural wines, IPA beers, on tap or bottled (all small craft productions), a couple of intriguing cocktails and some fancy, original sodas. There's something to suit any taste; even vegetarians are catered for. In addition, they offer a takeaway service and deliveries, with dishes from the menu and a sandwich that looks very much like a burger.

Their other address, MELT OBERKAMPF (74 Rue de la Folie, 75011 Méricourt), specialises in a central Mexican-style barbecue where their Texan Pitmaster, Jeffrey Howard, realises the traditional recipes of his homeland.

Address 83 Rue Legendre, 75017 Paris, +33 (0)1 9 87 09 99 25. Also at MELT OBERKAMPF, 74 rue de la Folie-Méricourt, 75011 Paris | **Getting there** Métro to La Fourche (Line 13); bus 66 | **Hours** Daily noon–3pm & 7.30–11pm (Sat & Sun open until 11.30pm) | **Tip** The charming Square des Batignolles, which is an English-style garden, an initiative of Napoleon III, is a bit further along the street after the church. It is one of the largest green spaces in this part of the city, designed in a natural English garden style – a great place to eat a MELT takeaway.

74__Mulino Mulè
The feel of flour

Just up the road from Cédric Casanova's first creation, La Tête dans les Olives (see ch. 104), is his latest invention, Mulino Mulè. Together with two friends, Marco Mulè and Roberto Rispoli, he's established a flour mill in the heart of the city! But it's not only a mill – it's a pasta factory, kitchen and restaurant combined!

Everything in the food chain, according to Casanova's rigorous principles, is not only traceable, but visible. You can see the magnificent wooden mill at the back of the shop, with its grinding wheels made of French granite. And next to the pasta machine you can admire the bronze discs used for extruding the different shapes, busiate, paccheri, caserecci, lasagne, rigatoni, gnocchetti sardi, fusilli, spaghettoni and liguine. You can buy the pasta freshly made or watch it being cooked if you're going to sit down for a meal.

The only thing you can't see is the wheat growing in the fields. But you *can* look at the grain before it goes into the mill – four carefully selected varieties of durum wheat, an ancient variety specially cultivated for making pasta, first mentioned by Aristotle nearly 2,500 years ago when he travelled in Sicily. And you can buy the freshly ground flour, sold by weight, in scoops from big sacks. And they sell the chapelure, the ground hard covering of the grain that you can use instead of breadcrumbs to make a batter, which smells marvellous.

The restaurant offers a set menu, or just one dish, if you prefer. The pasta is served in traditional wooden troughs, from which everyone shares, downed with Sicilian wines. The whole place is a delight – friendly and totally unpretentious. It's closed on Mondays, because that's milling day, when the miller has to pay attention. He can tell, he says, when the flour is ready by the sound that the millstones make, and the feel of the flour in his hands. Nothing could be more natural.

RIGATONI

BUSIATE

PACCHERI

CASERECCE

GNOCCHETTI
SARDI

SPAGHETTONI

FUSILLI

Address 25 Place Sainte-Marthe, 75010 Paris, +33 (0)9 54 75 92 07 | **Getting there** Métro to Goncourt (Line 3); bus 46 or 75 | **Hours** Tue–Sat 10am–11pm | **Tip** The Place Sainte-Marthe, a bit further on, is charming but unknown. Shaded by trees, this popular area is surrounded by many attractive bistros that become lively in the evening.

75__Nanashi

An exquisite mix of Japanese and French flavours

The Japanese chef Kaori Endo came to Paris and worked at the Rose Bakery before opening her first Nanashi in 2010.

The big idea of Nanashi is the traditional Japanese bento – the meal-in-one lunch box that was invented centuries ago for workers to take to the fields. Nanashi's bentos can be eaten on the spot or taken away. They combine oriental and occidental flavours in imaginative new ways. The contents are changed daily to keep regular customers coming back again and again. Three basic versions are on offer: the meat bento for example might contain a chicken breast cooked in breadcrumbs with tomato salsa and onion; the fish bento might contain a sea bass fillet cooked à la plancha with soy sauce and coriander. And there's always a vegetarian option, for example roasted sweet potatoes with citrus sauce and orange yoghurt sprinkled with pecans. For lighter bites, you can choose a miso soup with vegetables and tofu, an onigiri (rice ball with Kombu sesame seeds and capers) or a spring roll with chicken or vegetarian stuffing.

The desserts are similarly exotic fusions: on offer are vanilla and matcha (green tea), raspberry and chocolate cheesecake, or a matcha, raspberry and white chocolate loaf. With your meal you can drink the fresh fruit juice of the day (I had apple, pineapple, celery and basil), a banana and black sesame milkshake, or a rosemary, thyme and sage infusion.

Everything is cooked fresh, on the spot in the open kitchen. The fruit and the vegetables are all organic, as well as the cereals, seasoning, the eggs and the wine and most come from local producers. On Saturday and Sunday, Nanashi offers a kid's menu. The whole place has a family kitchen feel and though the sound level can get quite high, the atmosphere is relaxed and very Parisian. *Nanashi* means 'no name' in Japanese, but it's difficult to imagine an eating-place that is less anonymous.

Address 31 Rue de Paradis, 75010 Paris, +33 (0)1 40 22 05 55. Also at 57 Rue Charlot, 75003 Paris | **Getting there** Métro to Poissonnière (Line 7); bus 32 | **Hours** Mon–Fri noon–3pm & 7.30–11pm, Sat noon–4pm & 7.30–11pm, Sun noon–4pm | **Tip** The Rue de Paradis was once the street where you could buy all types of crystal, porcelain and other earthenware. Today, only a few such shops remain.

76_Nanina

Mozzarella made before your eyes

Nanina takes its name from the nickname of the Italian grandmother of Julien Carotenuto, the founder of this little cheese factory. It only opened in 2017 but now supplies cheeses to the Michelin-starred restaurant Septime in the Rue de Charonne.

The shop is unpretentious – a counter with a few Formica tables, a little terrace and, behind the high glass wall, the stainless-steel tanks where Julien and his right-hand man Franco Picciuolo work. The buffalo milk arrives twice a week from a co-operative of 400 animals in the Auvergne. But it is in the Rue de Basfroi that the cheeses are made every morning: mozzarella, burrata, ricotta, scarmoza (a variety of smoked mozzarella) and caciocavallo (a denser form given its name because the way in which the cheeses are tied looks like two saddlebags slung across the back of a horse). You can also buy other products and Italian charcuterie: mortadella, bresaola, spianata (a spicy salami), finocchiona (a salami made with fennel) and Parma ham. They also sell a few Italian wines, CaneNero craft beer and coffees.

You can nibble on the spot a cheese or charcuterie plate, or a handsome and very generous mixed plate with a bit of everything. The sandwiches are made with slightly toasted focaccia (from Da Rosa on the Rue de Seine): the caprese (with tomatoes, mozzarella and oregano), the mortadella (with pistachio, mortadella, ricotta and pepper), the bleu (with cooked ham and blue cheese), the spianata (salami with tomatoes and mozzarella), the bresaola (dried beef, scarmoza and dried tomatoes) and the parma (parma ham and mozzarella). For dessert there is ricotta with honey and walnuts; focaccia and nocciolata (hazelnut spread), and ricotta cheesecake.

The mozzarella is sold in 250g and 500g portions, and you have to eat it within 24 hours because it loses its delicious, delicate flavour if kept in the fridge for longer.

Address 24 bis Rue de Basfroi, 75011 Paris, +33 (0)7 78 46 46 36 | **Getting there**
Métro to Voltaire (Line 9); bus 61 or 69 | **Hours** Mon–Thu 10am–8.30pm, Fri & Sat
10am–10pm | **Tip** The house at no. 22 dates back to 1604 and is a rare example of a
working-class building of that time. It was fortunately saved from demolition in 2006.

77_Ô Divin

A mission to spread their love of eating

At the heart of Ô Divin lies the two brothers Rheda and Naoufel Zaïm's passion to share their love of eating and drinking with others. Everything they sell is what they love to eat and drink themselves. This is one of the most personal and wide-ranging food shops I've ever come across, and the selection is superb.

Their épicerie and wine cellar (converted from an old tripe shop) is stacked with culinary treasures: Pays Basque terrines and pâtés by Anne Rozès; Ardèche salami from the Salaisons Marion; semi-dried tomatoes from Gusto delle Puglia; gherkins from the Maison Marc (the last 100 per cent organic gherkins grown in France), Maldon salt flakes from the Blackwater estuary in Essex (a favourite of Jamie Oliver), English Luscombe and French Rigault fruit juices, jams by the Alsatian Christine Ferber, saucisse au couteau – sausages that are made with chunks cut with a knife, which are much tastier than those made with minced meat – and saucisse du paradis, made with a delicious kind of pepper called maniguette. And then there are all the spices, mustards, Banyuls vinegar, olive oil from Profil Grec (see ch. 93), Béton honey – so called because it's gathered from hives on the roofs of Saint-Denis (*béton* means 'concrete'), Prince de Paris ham, Périgord chicken, Pyrénées lamb… plus Deck & Donohue Montreuil beers and about 100 natural French and Italian wines. The bread comes from Bricheton (50 Rue de la Réunion). At no. 128, Ô Divin Primeur sells seasonal vegetables and fruit sourced from farmers in the Paris region (except for the exotics), dairy products and raw milk cheeses. And a bit further down at no. 118, there's the very recent Ô Divin Poisson.

The brothers' restaurant, at 66 Rue Guy Moquet is open Mon–Sat midday–2.30pm & 7.30–10.30pm, Sun midday–6.00pm. The cooking is simple, well executed, and the ambiance is quite delightful. They also do takeaway.

Address 130 Rue de Belleville, 75020 Paris, +33 (0)1 43 66 62 63. Also at 70 Rue
Saint-Blaise, 75020 Paris | **Getting there** Métro to Jourdain or Pyrénées (Line 11);
bus 26, 48, 60 | **Hours** Mon–Thu 9.30am–2.30pm & 4.30–9pm, Fri & Sat 9.30am–9pm,
Sun 9.30am–7pm | **Tip** At 213 Rue de Belleville you will find La Lanterne, a little stone
building dating from the 16th century that allows access to an underground aqueduct system,
one of the many along the Belleville Hill, which was an important water source for Paris.

78_ Pain de Sucre

Exquisite mouthfuls, both sweet and sour

Nathalie Robert and Didier Mathray both learned their art in top kitchens in France and abroad before working together for six years for the famous chef Pierre Gagnaire, a pioneer of fusion food. His motto *tourné vers demain mais soucieux d'hier* (face the future while respecting the past) inspired them when they decided to branch out on their own and open Pain de Sucre in 2004.

They offer individual cakes and larger ones to share. On the sweet side, the larger cakes include: the Rosemary (rosemary shortbread, rhubarb and raspberries, barley milk cream and chocolate); the Velours Noir (cacao biscuit with a hazelnut crust, cream and chocolate mousse); the Fresh Fruit Savarin (made with citrus syrup and seasonal fruits); the Corto (shortbread, raspberry purée and lemon confit, nasturtium biscuit, vanilla mousse and orange flowers). They offer tarts to share such as: the Pirouette (made with apple, blackcurrant and tangerine) and the Perle des Bois (almond shortbread, a vanilla cream and wild strawberries).

Their individual cakes include the Ephémère (coconut paste on a meringue base with blackcurrant jam, coconut cream and a layer of white chocolate) and the Bollywood (almond shortbread, pineapple jam and coriander cream). I adored this one almost as much as the Lili (nasturtium biscuit, black sesame crust, with a crème à la rose, raspberry purée and vanilla cream) and the Tatigala (almond shortbread, Madagascar vanilla mousseline cream, rosemary and caramelised apple).

On the salty side, they offer a whole range of bouchées (mouthfuls) and vérrines (little glassfuls) of savoury concoctions, together with mini focaccia sandwiches, spinach bread and different pains surprise (little sandwiches hidden in a loaf of bread), together with a vegetarian option, and various meat pies, one with snails. All of these delicacies you can eat on the spot, inside or out, or take away.

Address 14 Rue Rambuteau, 75003 Paris, +33 (0)1 45 74 68 92 | Getting there Métro to Étienne Marcel (Line 4); bus 29, 38 or 47 | Hours Thu–Mon 10am–8pm | Tip The extraordinary studio of the early modernist sculptor Constantin Brancusi, vividly reconstructed in the Place Georges Pompidou, makes for an unforgettable visit.

79__Paris Pêche

The freshest fish on the counter and the plate

Paris Pêche is an old family business, tracing its history back through several generations of Parisian fishmongers. Its first shop was in Montrouge, but in 1997 it expanded into the city centre. Lively displays on the counters show the best products from the fish markets of France and further afield: wild and organic bass, organic salmon, organic royal bream, swordfish, sumptuous tuna fillets to make sushi, little squids, a bizarre phenomenon called the daurade coryphène (the dolphin fish) or the mahi-mahi (a big tropical and subtropical fish, caught on a line). There's also a fine array of shellfish (cockles, clams and mussels), Gillardeau oysters, live spider crabs and lobsters in the tank.

On the prepared dishes counter: a poêlée du pêcheur ready to fry with plenty of fresh herbs; a spicy Mediterranean seafood salad; several taramas (plain, with pimento, sea urchins, scallops, crab, truffle); crab meat; brandade de morue (salt cod under a bed of potatoes), pike quenelles (fish dumplings – worth buying because they're very difficult to make); fresh wakame (a seaweed with a beautiful green colour); fresh sauces and soups. They also offer garnished seafood platters that you can order online.

A bit further on, at 79 Rue Crozatier, they have their Sea Bar, where you can enjoy six oysters and a glass of wine (+33 (0)1 43 47 45 47; daily 11.45am–12.15pm & 7–8pm). There is a set lunch menu and a choice of dishes on the blackboard: bass tartare with seaweed; oysters; moules marinières; whole oven-roasted bass with vegetables; tuna tataki, basmati rice and ponzu sauce; Saint Pierre fillet with pesto risotto; fresh tagliatelle with lobster and king prawns, and fresh lobster from Brittany grilled according to weight.

They also offer a regular menu with a whole choice of plates, some in the tapas style and about 10 desserts ranging from apple tart to chocolate mousse.

Address 17 Rue d'Aligre, 75012 Paris, +33 (0)1 43 43 12 11 | **Getting there** Métro to Ledru-Rollin or Faidherbe-Chaligny (Line 8); bus 57 or 86 | **Hours** Tue – Sat 8.30am – 1pm & 4 – 7.30pm, Sun 8.30am – 1.30pm; restaurant Tue – Sun midday – 2pm & 7 – 10.30pm | **Tip** At the corner of the Rue de Cotte and the Rue Théophile Roussel, there is a bakery with a beautiful Art Nouveau façade. The same street (as well as the Rue d'Aligre) leads to the Marché d'Aligre, one of the oldest in Paris (see ch. 69).

80 __Pastelaria Belem

Home baking, Portuguese-style

Founded 25 years ago, the Pastelaria Belem was the first Portuguese pâtisserie in Paris. It took its name from a famous old pâtisserie in Lisbon founded a century before. The Paris shop is smaller yet still celebrates everything that's Portuguese, from the traditional blue-and-white tiles to the glass case by the door containing the little figurines used to celebrate baptisms, communions and weddings in the Catholic ritual.

Here everything is home-made, including, of course, the pâtisseries, which are traditional Portuguese. On the sugary side, are the unmissable pasteis de nata – little egg custard flans sprinkled with cinnamon, absolutely delicious when they are fresh from the oven, the tigeladas (flans flavoured with lemon), the mimos (named after the warm hug a child gets from its mother) made with butter and coconut, flavoured with orange and topped with a glacé cherry, the bolas de Belem, a Portuguese version of the Berliner – a German doughnut stuffed with crème pâtissière, the tortas guardanapos – another cake stuffed with cream, and the Jesuitas (made with flaky pastry and finished with a meringue topping). To celebrate Epiphany, they make the traditional Bolo Rei – a large brioche garnished with glacé fruit.

On the salty side, there are paò com chouriço (chorizo bread), salgados (little pasties filled with fish or meat) and their own bread made with maize flour. They sell, in addition, a few grocery products, such as cheeses, sardines, orange or chestnut chocolates, heather and chestnut honey, coffee, quince jam, wines, fruit juices and port.

You can take away or eat on the spot in the cosy tearoom, while a large tortoiseshell cat sleeps peacefully in the sunny window. 'Here everything is like at home,' the very welcoming owner tells me as she insists I try another of her delicious pastries straight from the oven in the kitchen just behind.

Address 47 Rue Boursault, 75017 Paris, +33 (0)1 45 22 38 95 | **Getting there** Métro to Rome (Line 2); bus 53 or 66 | **Hours** Tue–Sun 8am–8pm | **Tip** At no. 62–64 there is a very fine Art Nouveau façade in stone, iron, brick and stoneware, designed in 1901 by René-Auguste Simonet and now listed as a historic monument.

81 La Pâtisserie du Meurice par Cédric Grolet

Where beauty deceives and taste delights

Cédric Grolet is famous for his friandises, fruit pastries that look like real fruit but aren't. You bite into a peach or pear, a strawberry or apple and discover it's a cake with a soft interior, often containing preserved fruit of the flavour of the fake exterior. His ambition is to make the taste of his pâtisseries as delicious as their appearance is beautiful.

After a brilliant career at Fauchon (the famous French delicatessen founded in 1886), Cédric Grolet (who was born in 1985) joined the team of the Meurice Hotel in 2011 and rapidly rose to become the Chef Pâtissier. In 2017, he was elected the best Chef Pâtissier in the world. In 2018, he opened a shop behind the hotel, as a public extension of his laboratoire de pâtisserie. The interior, designed by the architect team Ciguë, is long, pristine and totally white. When you arrive you can only see a few shelves with glass domes sheltering his fruit creations and several young pâtissier(e)s working hard behind the counter.

You have a choice between five cakes, in addition to Cédric's individual creations, such as a tarte chocolat, a peanut Paris-Brest and a sculpted tarte citron. These change regularly and are never the same as those in the Meurice at teatime. The cookies, the honey madeleines, made with honey from hives in the Paris area, and the gugelhupfs are available all day. Among Cédric's individual cakes you may find the Pomme Rouge (red apple), the Citron Noir (black lemon), and the Poire (pear). The production is limited. Once the last cake has been sold, the shop closes and you have to wait until the next day.

His large-scale cakes, such as his extraordinary Rubik's Cube, his Saint-Honoré and Tarte Aux Pommes have to be ordered in advance. The only drawback is that there is almost always a queue, which means you have to wait a long time.

Address 6 Rue de Castiglione, 75001 Paris, +33 (0)1 44 58 10 10 | **Getting there** Métro to Tuileries or Concorde (Line 1); bus 42, 52 or 68 | **Hours** Tue – Sun from midday | **Tip** The Place Vendôme, with the Vendôme Column erected by Napoleon I to commemorate the Battle of Austerlitz (1805), is surrounded by the most luxurious boutiques of the capital and the famous Ritz Hotel, where Princess Diana spent her last night.

82 Pâtisserie Jacques Genin
Where the unexpected and the exquisite meet

Jacques Genin is a wild cannon in the world of sweets, always experimenting yet always exquisite. Savouring one of his pâtes de fruits is like tasting perfectly ripe fruit exploding in your mouth: blackcurrants, lychee, raspberry, pear, pineapple, blood orange, rhubarb, mango and passion fruit. But then he also makes these sweets out of unexpected vegetables like beetroot, red pepper, fennel, carrot, celery, green tomato, pumpkin and cucumber – his invention seems endless. In what look like standard fudges you find nuts of all types, vanilla, liquorice, ginger and cinnamon. His chocolate tablets are flavoured with rare herbs and unusual spices. His individual chocolates have become famous for the balance of taste between the outer covering and inner soft filling. He has, single-handedly, opened whole new horizons in sweet making and tasting.

Jacques Genin is as adventurous with the past as he is with the future, reviving popular cakes, which have long been dismissed as old fashioned. His big classic – the divine Paris-Brest – is unique. The cake was created in 1910 by Louis Durand to commemorate the iconic cycle race from Paris to Brest and back. It is a crown of puff pastry of perfect texture sliced horizontally in two and filled with a praline flavoured crème pâtissière and topped with grilled hazelnuts. Eat it at once, because the pastry has to be crisp.

Genin was wild from the beginning. He left school at 13 to work in an abattoir. The arc of his career from such unlikely beginnings has been extraordinary. Since 2008, he has established his business in a superb workshop and boutique, where you can taste the delicacies while sipping tea or coffee at tables and in armchairs, though, be warned, the takeaway cakes have to be ordered a day in advance. The atmosphere is exquisite but not exclusive. At Genin's, the best is not too good for anyone.

Address 133 Rue de Turenne, 75003 Paris, +33 (0)1 45 77 29 01 | Getting there
Métro to Filles du Calvaire (Line 8); bus 29 or 96 | Hours Tue–Sun 11am–7pm, Sat
11am–7.30pm | Tip All along the Rue de Turenne you can admire the façades of some
beautiful old town houses. At no. 41 you will find the Fontaine de Joyeuse (1847), in
which there is a bronze sculpture of a young child holding a jug that pours its water
into a large shell.

83 Pâtisserie Stohrer

The home of the rum baba

When Louis XV married the daughter of King Stanislav of Poland, he got more than he bargained for – or perhaps that was his secret plan – for her father's favourite pâtissier, the Alsatian Nicolas Stohrer, decided to follow the princess to France. Five years later, in 1730, Stohrer opened his own cake shop in the city, delighted with the Parisian reception of his art.

Stohrer's success was not just due to his remarkable skills but also to his imagination. One day King Stanislav brought home a dry Polish brioche. Stohrer, not wanting to throw the miserable object away, soaked it in Malaga wine and perfumed it with saffron. Then he added a crème pâtissière, sprinkled with raisins and fresh grapes. The king was so delighted that he named it after his favourite book, *One Thousand and One Nights* – and called it Ali Baba. So, after many minor transformations, the rum baba was born. Nowadays, the Maison Stohrer produces three versions of this world-famous dessert, and I recommend that you try them all, though not perhaps at the same time.

Another house speciality is the puits d'amour (wells of love) of which the first recipe dates back to 1735. The actual version created by Nicholas Stohrer is a puff pastry with a coating of vanilla crème pâtissière, caramelised with a hot iron. Among other unique products is their tarte Chibouste: a layer of apples, flambéed with calvados, on a bed of puff pastry, topped with a souffléed carmelised crème. Stohrer was also famous for his gugelhupf (a traditional Alsatian brioche paste with raisins and almonds), which is still sold at the shop today. If you want traditional cakes, without the fuss of modern embellishments, Stohrer's is the place.

The shop is worth a visit for itself, since it's now a listed, historic building. Its décor dates back to 1864, enlivened by glass panels designed by the famous decorative painter Paul-Jacques Baudry.

Address 51 Rue Montorgueil, 75002 Paris, +33 (0)1 42 33 38 20 | **Getting there**
Métro to Sentier (Line 3); bus 20, 29, 39 or 72 | **Hours** Daily 7.30am–8.30pm | **Tip**
Stroll through the Passage du Grand Cerf, with its boutiques, which leads to the Place
Goldoni, where the great Italian playwright died in 1793.

84 __ Patrick Roger Chocolat

A Rodin among chocolate makers

Entering one of Patrick Roger's dark shops is like walking into a tropical forest. Green and black is the theme. You are faced with a back wall of emerald-green glass panels lit from behind. All the other walls are black. What's most striking are the huge dark sculptures standing on the glass table in the centre. You feel as though you're in an art gallery, not a shop, looking at the work of a Rodin of the jungle. It's a while before you realise that these extraordinary creations are made of chocolate, and the green boxes all around are full of chocolates too. You are, believe it or not, in a chocolate shop.

The staff in Patrick Roger's shops love to tell the story of their famous chocolatier. His tongue-in-cheek playfulness is particularly French. To celebrate the 50th anniversary of the May '68 Revolution, he made stone cobbles out of praline and almonds with whole almonds inside – cobblestones were the weapons the revolutionaries dug up from the roads to throw at the police. At Christmas, he makes chocolate oranges garnished with almonds, because old people in France used to be famous for complaining that the young were spoilt with too many presents, when all *they* got for Christmas was an orange. Why so many almonds? Because Patrick Roger owns almond fields near Perpignan.

What you take away are the chocolates, and these are superb. His chocolate bars are ranked from the strongest to the sweetest: 80 per cent cocoa from Cuba, Ecuador, Tanzania, Madagascar, Papua New Guinea, Brazil and Venezuela. His individual chocolates are exquisite, with a remarkable range of surprising tastes, such as ganache lemon grass / peppermint, almond paste / chestnut and oat / Séchuan pepper truffle. The takeaway experience is as surprising as being in the shop. Patrick Roger now runs nine boutiques in Paris and the region, and one in Brussels, all as beautiful as the others.

Address 43 Rue des Archives, 75003 Paris, +33 (0)9 61 68 39 30 | **Getting there** Métro to Hôtel de Ville (Line 1 or 11); bus 29 or 75 | **Hours** Daily 10.30am–7.30pm | **Tip** At no. 62, in the Hôtel de Guénégaud built by François Mansart in the 17th century, you will find the Musée de la Chasse et de la Nature, which displays the relationship between mankind and animals over the ages through the customs and traditions of hunting.

85__Peonies

Bouquets of flowers and aromatic beverages

Peonies is the imaginative creation of Clémentine Lévy, a well-known model, media presenter and DJ, who named her unique shop after her favourite flower. She trained as a barista – a specialist in beverages based on coffee – and then as a florist to enable her to realise her dream of opening a coffee shop selling flowers in a busy commercial street in the heart of Paris. This untried venture was, to say the least, a risky business. But – bravo! – it's been a great success. Peonies is like a bubble of fresh air in the middle of the tough city.

Peonies' bouquets are charming – an imaginative mixture of cultivated flowers, wild meadow flowers and grasses, reminiscent of the bunches one picked as a child in the countryside. You can choose a ready-made bouquet or create one of your own, or attend one of the workshops on how to make bouquets that will charm your friends.

As for food, everything is veggie. For savoury dishes she offers grilled cheese with baby spinach leaves, open sandwiches with avocado and cocoa nibs, a small or large salad of the day, rolls of the day, and (only on Sundays) Oeuf Cocotte de Tom with a side dish. All the vegetables, naturally, are seasonal.

For something sweet she offers flavoured loaves, home-made granola with fromage blanc and fresh fruit and organic matcha tea pancakes. Drinks include coffee (espresso, noisette with a drop of milk, latte, cappuccino), V60 – a Japanese filter coffee technique – chai – tea as made in India, which can be latte, matcha or organic latte – organic tea, fresh fruit juice of the day, elderflower or lime and lemongrass lemonade, iced coffee latte with optional lavender syrup, and almond milk. They also sell organic coffee, handmade cups, Kinto brand teapots, T-shirts and tote bags. All this is presented in delightful surroundings, with pretty décor of green tiles and terrazzo tables, and flowers everywhere.

Address 81 Rue du Faubourg Saint-Denis, 75010 Paris | **Getting there** Métro to Château d'Eau (Line 6); bus 35, 38, 39, 46 or 65 | **Hours** Tue–Fri 9am–7.30pm, Sat 10.30am–7.30pm, Sun 10.30am–4.30pm | **Tip** At no. 16, the Restaurant Julien, which was once a bouillon, is now a very chic brasserie, but it hasn't changed its fine Art Deco façade and interior. It is now listed as a historic monument.

86__Le Petit Keller

Japanese and French cuisine meet on a side street

This place is a hidden gem. It's in an unlikely street, with genuine 50s décor, original tiles and old Formica tables. But the natural charm and exceptional food is immediately captivating. Naturalness is the key. Scrawled across the window is their creed: 'natural wines and products, take away bento at lunch'. Kaori Endo took a bold step opening this new place, a fusion of Japanese and French cuisine, but the result is a totally unpretentious triumph.

Almost all the ingredients are organic. On the menu are big dishes to share: filet of bream à la séchuanaise with green cabbage and broccoli; grilled beef 350g à la plancha, teriyaki sauce, rice in garlic oil and green salad. For individual dishes, she offers: saucisse sèche by from Emmanuel Chavassieux (which are among the best in the world); nitamago egg (marinated in rapadura and tamarisk); Champignons de Paris cooked in olive oil and garlic; adzuki bean hummus (made with Japanese red beans); fried vegetables marinated in dashi and ginger; Japanese omelette with fresh spinach and sesame; mackerel sashimi with cashew nut cream and pickled red onions; cockle salad with black rice and vegetables with curry coconut cream; crab salad with fennel, cucumber, samphire and fresh nori seaweed; beef tataki with aromatic salad; organic salmon tataki with white miso seasoning; grilled Spanish pork pluma (a cut of meat that, once tasted, is never forgotten) with dates and celery salsa.

The desserts are as delicious, taken after the meal, or served separately at teatime: a spongy matcha tea loaf; a bitter chocolate mousse with chocolate crumble, dates and passion fruit; blueberry tart with pecan nuts; pavlova with rhubarb and red berries; adzuki purée, apricot, whipped cream, oat crumble, matcha and almonds. The natural wines are chosen by Kaori Endo's husband Mikael Lemasle of Crus et Découvertes (see ch. 33).

Address 13 bis Rue Keller, 75011 Paris, +33 (0)1 43 55 90 54 | Getting there Métro to Ledru-Rollon (Line 8); bus 61, 69 or 76 | Hours Tue–Fri noon–2.45pm & 7.30–10.30pm, Sat 12.30–3.30pm & 7.30–10.30pm | Tip At 116 Avenue Ledru-Rollin there's an ancient brasserie, Le Bistrot du Peintre, with its old wooden façade and Art Nouveau interior, which is classified as a historic monument.

87 _ Petrossian

The mystique of caviar

Melkoum and Mouchegh Petrossian, two Armenian brothers and refugees, founded their company in Paris in the early 1920s. Mouchegh was married to the daughter of a trader in top-quality caviar, and this connection enabled them to introduce into Paris the Caviar Malossol, one of the best in the world made from whole sturgeon eggs, preserved in minimal salt (in Russian, *Malossol* means 'lightly salted'). This caviar was then almost unknown in Paris and became a sensation. Petrossian have never lost their pre-eminence in this market, nor their connections with their suppliers in Russia.

In the 1930s, the brothers added smoked salmon and then Maviar® (smoked cod eggs, a delicacy exclusive to Petrossian) and Royal Crab. The original shop on the Boulevard de la Tour-Maubourg offers along with many different caviars, a large choice of smoked fish eggs, poutargue – a dried and salted egg sack of mullet or tuna, foie gras, several tarama (including the famous Maviar® Tamara) and Russian specialities such as pirozhkis, Russian herrings, Tsar salad, Petrossian Caesar salad, soft boiled eggs with caviar, croque-monsieur with caviar and veal sliced with tuna sauce and caviar, chocolate pearls with vodka, cognac or caramel, and, of course, a whole range of vodkas.

At the Petrossian restaurant, at no. 13, caviar is king – or rather the Tsar. The set menu Caviar Absolument is for real enthusiasts, and offers tastings of different types of caviar with simple toast or blinis. Also on offer are French fries or pommes soufflées (fiendishly difficult to make) to dunk in liquid caviar, which are the summit of regressive pleasure.

The shop at the Boulevard de Courcelles offers a similar range of products together with a snack restaurant providing upmarket street food such as sandwiches with beluga sturgeon, prepared in a pastrami way, or a Royal Crab roll with celeriac.

Address 13 Boulevard de la Tour-Maubourg, 75007 Paris, +33 (0)1 44 11 32 22. Also at 106 Boulevard de Courcelles, 75017 Paris, +33 (0)1 47 66 16 16 | **Getting there** Métro to Invalides (Line 8 or 13); bus 28 or 69 | **Hours** Mon – Sat 9.30am – 8pm, restaurant daily 12.30 – 2.30pm & 7.30 – 10.30pm | **Tip** Visit the Musée des Invalides, created by Louis XIV, on La Place des Invalides, containing the magnificently simple tomb of Napoleon I, as well as the Musée des Plans-Reliefs, which houses a collection of models of fortified cities used for military purposes.

88 Picnic at Versailles

A taste of royal luxury on the grass

The park and gardens of Versailles were designed by André Le Nôtre and completed by Jules Hardouin-Mansart in the 17th century to glorify the Sun King, Louis XIV. They spread over a vast 2,000 acres, which means that nowadays there's room for everyone.

The park is separated from the formal gardens by two huge waterways, the Grand Canal and the Pièce d'Eau des Suisses. Picnics in the park have become immensely popular with Parisians. They are now authorised in two places: on the Plaine Saint-Antoine near the Château de Trianon and along the Pièce d'Eau des Suisses, facing the Orangerie. Access is provided to these picnic areas not through the Palace of Versailles but through the Rue de l'Indépendance Américaine or the Grille des Matelots.

Take advantage of this historical setting to put aside, just for once, the awful, modern plastic-coated cool boxes, which have become the standard way of carrying food but that make it lose all taste. Choose instead a traditional basket, and put in your bottles of rosé or white wine (in those sleeves that are so effective in keeping it cool) and your tarts, terrines, salads, fruit, cheeses and bread, which all need fresh air to keep them flavoursome. Then select your spot in the open or under the shade of one of the many, great spreading trees, spread your cloth on the grass, open your hamper and first bottle, and begin to enjoy some of the best hours of your life. If you need entertainment, ball games and badminton are allowed, and boats can be hired on the Grand Canal. The lawns are so vast that this is the ideal place to organise convivial gatherings of all your friends.

The park's opening hours can change, which means it's best to check on the internet before going. On Saturdays in summer the gardens close at 5.30pm for waterfall displays, which you have to pay to see. Otherwise, this taste of royal luxury is free.

Address Château de Versailles, Place d'Armes, 78000 Versailles | **Getting there** RER (C), station Versailles Rive Gauche or take a train from Montparnasse station and get off at Versailles Chantiers | **Hours** Check on the internet | **Tip** Needless to say, while you are there it's worth visiting the Château, the Trianons and the Potager du Roi, built between 1678 and 1683 by Jean-Baptiste de La Quintinie to provide for the royal table.

89__Pierre Hermé
The haute-couture pâtissier

Pierre Hermé says 'pleasure is his only guide.' This joyful spirit has enabled him to revolutionise French pâtisserie. He replaced traditional fussy decorations with contemporary elegant designs. By using, as he says, 'sugar like salt – i.e. as a seasoning that helps to reveal other nuances of taste,' he revolutionised the taste of cakes. Then he makes daring, at times crazy, combinations of flavours – macarons made with caviar or foie gras. And the revolution continues because Hermé is always developing new recipes.

One of his star pâtisseries (illustrated) is called l'Ispahan. It's a large macaron that brings together the tastes of raspberry, lychee and rose. He has reinterpreted this combination as a loaf cake, a croissant, a Paris-Brest, a baba, a tart, a mille-feuille, a cheese cake, and a sorbet of marvellous subtlety. Also try his Tarte Infiniment Vanille, Tarte Infiniment Café or his Chou Infiniment Citron – the 'infiniment' is earned because you'll never taste vanilla or coffee or lemon so definitively. Let yourself be tempted too by the Ultime, with dark chocolate and vanilla, the 2000 Feuilles, with praline and hazelnut, or the Cerise sur le Gâteau – which is literally the cherry on the cake.

Pierre Hermé springs from four generations of Alsatian boulangers-pâtissiers. At 14, he left his family to learn from the great pastry chef Gaston Lenôtre. Then he worked for François Clerc and Alain Passard, at Fauchon, then for Ladurée. In 1996, he created Maison Pierre Hermé, with his associate Charles Znaty, and opened his first shop not in Paris but in Tokyo. In 2000, he came back to France and opened his first Parisian pâtisserie on the Rue Bonaparte. Nowadays, there are Pierre Hermé shops all over the world. He's earned accolades everywhere, but perhaps the best tribute was *Vogue* magazine's when it dubbed him the 'Picasso of Pastry'.

Address 72 Rue Bonaparte, 75006 Paris, +33 (0)1 43 54 47 77 | **Getting there** Métro to Saint Sulpice (Line 4); bus 39 or 95 | **Hours** Sun–Thu 10am–7pm, Fri & Sat 10am–8pm | **Tip** In l'Église Saint-Sulpice, one of the biggest in Paris, and constructed in the 17th century on the foundations of a 12th-century church, don't miss Eugène Delacroix's magnificent late painting *Jacob Wrestling with the Angel*.

90 _ Poilâne
Farm bread in the city

Pierre Poilâne opened his first bakery on the Rue du Cherche-Midi in 1932, defying the modern trend for manufactured, white bread. He employed strictly traditional methods, using only stoneground flour and sourdough for natural fermentation. All his loaves were made by hand, including kneading, and cooked in a wood-fired oven. The farm loaf had returned to the city.

His son, Lionel, took over the business in 1970. He maintained his father's principles, with the exception of introducing machine kneading. The wheat is carefully selected to be without pesticides, and ground on stone mill wheels leaving some of the wheat bran, which gives the flour its dark hue. No enhanced flavourings are added at the kneading stage, apart from sea salt, which is the best – sel de Guerande. The fermentation with natural yeasts is slow and it is this that gives Poilane bread its distinctive sour taste, which became famous throughout Paris, and then the world. Since the 1970s, 24 wood ovens have been crackling at Bièvres, shipping thousands of loaves around the globe.

The variety of breads is limited on purpose to the *miche* (a large round yeast loaf), bread with walnuts, rye bread, rye bread with raisins, and pepper bread. In addition, the bakery produces its range of viennoiseries: croissants, brioches, pains au chocolat, chaussons (apple turnovers), fruit tarts and flans. It also sells a few other products such as Christine Ferber's famous jams from Alsace.

Next to the bakery, a café lets you taste their products, for breakfast and an all-day menu: toasted bread with butter and jam, Bircher – a muesli made with cereal flakes, oat-milk and fresh fruit – oeuf en cocotte with toasted brioche, cheddar and a green salad, or peppered bread with avocado and egg. To drink there is a vast choice of beverages and wines by the glass. Poilâne also has a bakery and café in London.

Address 8 Rue du Cherche-Midi, 75006 Paris, +33 (0)1 45 48 42 59. Also at 49 Boulevard de Grenelle, 75015 Paris | **Getting there** Métro to Sèvres-Babylone (Line 10 or 12); bus 39, 70 or 87 | **Hours** Daily 7am–8.30pm; le Comptoir Mon–Sat 8.30am–7pm, Sun 9.30am–3.30pm | **Tip** At the Carrefour de la Croix-Rouge stands César's enormous soldered bronze sculpture, entitled *Le Centaure*.

91 La Poissonnerie du Dôme

The freshest wild fish

The Poissonnerie du Dôme specialises in providing the freshest wild fish caught, much of it by line, along the French coast. According to the season you'll find many rare specialities: large prawns from Saint-Gilles-Croix-de-Vie; wild salmon from the Adour along with elvers (baby eels), that are caught when they return from the sea to swim up rivers inland; groper and bass fished on the line from Concarneau; langoustine royale from Audierne; lobster from Roscoff; tiny red mullet fry from the Turballe; royal bream from Loctudy; the big crabs of Camaret-sur-Mer; scallops from the harbour of Brest; and one of the rarest delicacies of all Demoiselles de Cherbourg – little lobsters that are caught when their skins are still soft after casting their hard shells – from the Chausey Islands, to name only a few.

Jean-Pierre Lopez, master of the shop, ensures that all his fish are of exceptional freshness, still bright-eyed, with the firm flesh that distinguishes wild fish from the flaccid versions reared in farms. It's no wonder that the shop is the supplier to the most famous restaurants in Paris, like L'Ambroisie of Bernard Pacaud, L'Astrance of Pascal Barbot and the restaurant owned by David Toutain. And it became the official supplier of L'Elysée Palace during the presidencies of Mitterrand and Chirac.

The staff are immaculately professional and always eager to help, even when a little girl when I was there wanted a couple of grams of fish for a pizza. The staff prepare the fish according to your needs, whether whole, filleted, sliced or diced specially for Japanese sashimi or tartares, the French equivalent of raw fish dishes. The prices, obviously, reflect the quality of the product. And the shop itself is a delight to visit. Opened in 1987, it's decorated in beautiful tiles representing fish and seafood, designed by the famous artist Slavik.

Address 4 Rue Delambre, 75014 Paris, +33 (0)1 43 35 23 95. Also at 61 Rue Damrémont, 75018 Paris, +33 (0)1 42 64 17 04 | **Getting there** Métro to Vavin (Line 4); bus 58, 68, 82 or 91 | **Hours** Tue–Sat 8am–1pm & 4–7pm, Sun 8am–1pm | **Tip** Visit the nearby cemetery of Montparnasse, containing the tombs of many famous people, including Jean-Paul Sartre, Simone de Beauvoir and Samuel Beckett. All the names are listed on a map at the entrance. There is also a beautiful sculpture by Niki de Saint Phalle on the tomb of one of her friends.

92 Pralus

The purest chocolate from plant to bar

François Pralus was born with a chocolate spoon in his mouth. His father was a master pâtissier in Roanne, where his son honed his remarkable skills. He then decided to make chocolates in a totally new way. Most chocolatiers buy in their basic ingredients, but François was determined to exercise quality control over the whole process, from bean to bar. He now only uses beans carefully chosen from America, Africa and from plantations around the Indian Ocean.

He has created about 20 new crus of chocolate – a term taken from the wine business, meaning high-quality wine from a particular terroir – as well as three blends, a 45 per cent milk chocolate and a 100 per cent criollo from Madagascar, where he runs a plantation of cocoa plants.

A good way to enter his world is to taste his Pyramide des Tropiques, a selection of 10 different chocolate squares. Then try his Barre Infernale, a delicious praline bar filled with almonds or hazelnuts, which comes in different flavours. Then tackle his sumptuous Cubissime, a praline cube with ground hazelnuts, almonds and pistachios, wrapped in dark chocolate and covered with gold leaf. He makes 18 different chocolate bars, a cocoa infusion, made from chocolate nibs, a Piemontese hazelnut cream and a grilled Valencia almond cream, which you can use as a spread on bread or taste on the spoon as a treat! His Le Carré de Café® is a real discovery; it's made from 100 per cent Arabica coffee from Brazil, which you bite into like chocolate.

Not forgetting the icon of his establishment: the sublime Praluline®, baked in the shop. In 1955, François' father, Auguste, made a brioche with pink pralines that is now famous across the world. The praline chips, which make it so special, are made with hazelnuts and almonds coated with pink boiled sugar which is then broken into pieces. Some of his shops sell as many as 1,000 on a Saturday.

Address 1 Rue de l'Ancienne-Comédie, 75006 Paris, +33 (0)1 43 29 10 37. Also at 35 Rue Rambuteau, 75004 Paris, 9 Rue Bachaumont, 75002 Paris and 44 Rue Cler, 75007 Paris | **Getting there** Métro to Odéon (Line 4); bus 58, 63, 70, 86, 87 or 96 | **Hours** Mon 10am–1pm & 2–7.30pm, Tue–Sat 10.30am–8pm, Sun 10am–6pm | **Tip** The Rue de Seine, with its beautiful old town houses, is packed with some of the most interesting, and exclusive, antique shops and art galleries in Paris.

93__Profil Grec
Greek olive orchards with women's names

The little headquarters of Profil Grec serves as a tasting centre for professional chefs, an office/kitchen for its staff and a tiny épicerie. Everyone is welcome because this is the nerve centre of a mission. Profil Grec has existed since 2015, but the idea of selling the exceptional olive oils of Kalamata in Greece was hatched in the mind of Alexandre Rallis in 2009.

The district around Kalamata has, since ancient times, been famous for its olives, which are grown in very dry, stony ground, often on very small, distinct parcels of land. This terrain gives the oil its special taste and mineral bite. But Alexandre Rallis recognised that these tastes vary, not just from field to field, but from year to year. He had the bright idea of making and marketing olive oil from these distinct localities and years. He was especially interested in local traditions of harvesting where they survived; all of his olives are hand picked, and the flavours vary greatly according to whether they are picked early or late in the season. Then he named each little orchard after a woman, starting with his mother and grandmother, then widening out to include many women he admired. He sells these named varieties of oil in five-litre cans, or individually bottled if the year is a vintage one.

Profil Grec also sells its own olive paste, made exclusively from Kalamata olives, much tastier than the standard tapenade. It stocks a few other local specialities, such as Mr Memmos' feta cheese, which is soft and delicious, sfela, a matured feta, saganaki, a cheese that you eat fried with fig jam, and an exceptional bottarga, a dried fish roe from Mr Trikalinos, which is soft and hardly salted.

You can pop in to Profil Grec for a bottle of olive oil or buy their oils in the shops of Hugo Desnoyer, Ô Divin and Terroir d'Avenir, all of which are mentioned in this guide. And you can order online.

Address 7 Rue de Savies, 75020 Paris, +33 (0)9 72 86 07 22 | Getting there Métro to Pyrénées (Line 11); bus 26 or 96 | Hours Mon–Fri 2–7pm | Tip Wander around the quarter with its very charming little streets, which have a village flavour.

94__RAP
A shining star among Italian grocers

Alessandra Pierini has an overriding passion in her life: the finest Italian groceries. She first opened an Italian restaurant, Pasta e Dolce, in Marseilles then moved to Paris where she opened RAP – the Restaurant Alessandra Pierini alongside a delicatessen grocery. Now she has abandoned the restaurant, to concentrate all her (considerable) energies and expertise on her main love – the finest food products of Italy. She knows the country like the back of her hand and has searched everywhere for the tastiest produce, often made in very small batches by local producers. She is in love with the idea of 'terroir' – how the local environment affects the taste of produce – and the result is her small but densely packed shop, stacked from floor to ceiling with exquisite items.

Here you will find the very best balsamic vinegars, aged naturally in barrels, without the addition of artificial colouring, which gives the cheaper imitations their awful, smothering taste. She stocks Pastiglie Leone (pastilles made with real fruit essences), several products of the sea, such as tuna, poutargue (dried mullet roe) and anchovies, as well as many standard Italian products like tinned tomatoes, tomato purée, polenta, panettone and Carnaroli, Arborio and Venere rice. She has many specialities like Sicilian almonds, taggiasca olives and Genovese pesto. And among all this abundance, there is a choice display of cheeses and charcuterie, and on racks above, fine Italian wines (some organic), limoncellos and grappas.

At the entrance, a few baskets of fresh vegetables, fruits and herbs (including the indispensable basil) give you a whiff of Italy as you leave. Alessandra also writes recipe books published by Les Éditions de l'Épure, my favourite cookbook publisher. Her enthusiasm inspires everything, including her staff. Rarely have I left a shop feeling more welcome.

Address 4 Rue Fléchier, 75009 Paris, +33 (0)1 42 80 09 91 | **Getting there** Métro to Notre-Dame-de-Lorette (Line 12); bus 26, 32, 43, 67 or 74 | **Hours** Tue–Sat 10.30am–7.30pm, Sun 10am–1pm | **Tip** Just nearby is Notre-Dame-de-Lorette, known to be the most colourful church in Paris. Constructed under the reigns of Louis XVIII and Louis-Philippe, it is neoclassical in style.

95 La REcyclerie

From old railway station to ecological eatery

La petite ceinture (the little belt), the old railway that used to run right round Paris, was finished in 1867 but abandoned in 1937. There's still fierce debate about what to do with its remains. La REcyclerie had the happy idea of turning one of its old stations, the Ornano, into a centre for practical ecology. Here you can eat, meet and get help with repairing things, revitalising your life in every sustainable way. In the canteen, which fills the light, airy space of the old station hall, you order at the counter and then sit down with a disc, which rings when your food, freshly cooked, is ready to collect. When you're finished, you recycle the remains yourself in the different bins provided.

You have a choice between the set menu of the day, three vegetarian dishes (pasta, vegetarian stir-fry or a risotto) or a burger (a nourishing spicy beef wrap served with home-made French fries). From 3 to 5pm, afternoon tea is served with pâtisseries. Every Thursday the menu becomes totally vegetarian and vegan. Wine is siphoned from tapped containers but they have also excellent draught beers and fruit juices. Near the entrance, they sell dishes to take away: watermelon and lime gazpacho; attiéké (fermented cassava semolina) with peppers, onion, garlic and parsley; bún bò – a Vietnamese dish with beef, rice noodles, cucumber, shallots, garlic, onion, lettuce, mint and Thai basil.

On Saturdays, Sundays and public holidays you can enjoy brunch, including a vegetarian one, either savoury or sweet, comprising home-made tabbouleh, crunchy salad, coleslaw, scrambled eggs, or rice pudding, chestnut streusel, pineapple salad, with mint syrup.

Outside there's a little paradise that runs along the old railway track: a small urban farm, with chickens and ducks, vegetable beds and fruit, and plenty of cosy nooks, armchairs and couches where you can eat, read or canoodle.

Address 75 Boulevard Ornano, 75018 Paris, +33 (0)1 42 57 58 49 | **Getting there** Métro to Porte de Clignancourt (Line 4); bus 56 or 85 | **Hours** Mon–Thu noon–midnight, Fri & Sat noon–2am, Sun 11am–10pm | **Tip** On the other side of the *périphérique*, the Paris ring road, at about 100 metres, there is the St Ouen flea market – one of the biggest and best in the city.

96 _ Rose Bakery

A pre-Brexit mix of English and French cuisine

Rose Carrarini first worked in fashion, but then turned to food. She opened a delicatessen with her husband Jean-Charles, and a restaurant in London in 1988. But her first real success came when she, cheekily, opened a bakery in Paris, christening it with her name. How could a South African brought up in England survive among the greatest bakers in France and, many would say, the world? But her cooking, which was simple, refreshing and organic, conquered the capital overnight. There's a real Rose bakery spirit – warm, welcoming and contagious. In its original location on the Rue des Martyrs, this generous spirit was present in the design, on one side a takeaway and on the other a tearoom and canteen.

Two counters face each other: one savoury, the other sweet. On the savoury side are seasonal tarts and vegetable or polenta quiches. There are tempting pizzas and cereal salads (you have a choice between six or seven, all equally mouthwatering), cooked dishes and cold or hot soups. On the sweet side, the white loaves are magnificent: a traditional marbled one with chocolate (which looked exactly like my mother's), and others flavoured with lemon / orange, red berries, banana, carrot and pistachio. Some are gluten-free and look so luscious you want to eat a slice at once. There's a delicious cheesecake and a superb Eton mess (a merry blend of strawberries, crushed meringue and whipped cream) – her English upbringing surfacing with a vengeance. To drink, they sell the delicious ginger and elderflower cordials of the Belvoir Fruit Farms. On Sundays they serve brunch, but come early to avoid the queue.

Rose Bakery now has several addresses in Paris, among them a tearoom in Bon Marché and another at the Musée de la Vie Romantique, a charming place with a very romantic garden. And her success has travelled the world: Rose Bakery is now in New York, Tokyo and Seoul.

Address 46 Rue des Martyrs, 75009 Paris, +33 (0)1 42 82 12 80 | **Getting there** Métro to Saint-Georges (Line 12); bus 30, 54 or 67 | **Hours** Daily 9.30am – 8.30pm | **Tip** At no. 9 you can see an amazing neo-Gothic-style building which was, until 1946, a private (members only) brothel specialising in sadomasochism.

97 La Rue du Nil
A little gathering of excellence

Most of the shops along this tiny street are run by Terroirs d'Avenir. 'Terroir' doesn't just mean land in French, but encompasses the whole ancient tradition of local production – the tastes of wines, vegetables and fruits grown on particular soils under particular climatic conditions and the animals that are reared on this terrain. 'Terroirs d'Avenir' implies the future of this whole way of food production in France. It is a vision of hope, not just a name.

Alexandre Drouard and Samuel Nahon founded Terroirs d'Avenir in 2008. Inspired by the Slow Food Movement and by Alexandre's father, a renowned food historian, they wanted to find an answer to a simple question: why can't you buy locally produced food at reasonable prices in big cities? They uncovered a complex world of small breeders but realised that they'd have to establish their own supply chain. They began by delivering produce themselves to restaurants, and were soon patronised by famous chefs like Sven Chartier.

Between 2012 and 2015 they opened a greengrocer's, butcher's, fishmonger's and baker's along the Rue du Nil, all following the same strict ethics: only selling produce grown in open fields, pork of at least 12 months old, and chicken between 110 and 120 days. Today they buy everything direct from producers. They work with 250 breeders and farmers whom they each know personally. The care taken from soil to shop is manifest in the rich, delicious tastes of everything they sell.

The Terroirs d'Avenir shops are just steps away from Frenchie's Restaurant and Frenchie To Go, which serve Greg Marchand's brilliantly inventive dishes and sandwiches. And between them is Hyppolite Courtois' store. He created the famous l'Arbre à Café brand, and if you're lucky, and the staff are there, and not on errands round the world, they serve his delicious coffee to people in the street. La Rue du Nil is a treat.

Address In the 2nd Arrondissement between Rue Montorgueil and Rue d'Aboukir |
Getting there Métro to Sentier (Line 3); bus 8, 9, 20, 29 or 39 | **Hours** Check the website
www.terroirs-avenir.fr for details | **Tip** See the vertical garden at 83 Rue d'Aboukir,
designed by Patrick Blanc, the great French originator of modern hanging gardens.

98__ Sacha Finkelsztajn

Celebrating Jewish Ashkenazi culinary traditions

The shop is simply called the 'Boutique Jaune' by Parisians, among whom it has become something on an institution. It was created immediately after World War II in 1946 by Itzik and Dora Finkelsztajn – one of the first signs of positive regeneration after the terrible period of the Nazi occupation. It is now the quintessential centre of Russian and Central European cuisine in the capital, the epitome of the Jewish Ashkenazi culinary tradition.

All the classics are here. There's traditional cumin bread; the Razowy, bread made with wholemeal rye and yeast; the Rogalik, made with cumin and fried onions; bagels, plaits of bread sprinkled with poppy or sesame seeds; matselehs, crunchy pancakes with onions, sesame, salt or poppy seeds; pletzels, round buns with onions. It's with the last that they make their delicious sandwiches garnished with aubergine or pepper caviar, with pastrami, pickles, turkey, tomato and cucumber.

The sweet side is a real *farandole* (a country dance where everyone joins in). There are strudels, made with apple, almond, raisins, preserved orange peel and cinnamon; the Makowiec, a Polish rolled cake with poppy seeds, and numerous cheesecakes. There's the Vatrouchka with vanilla and raisins; the Sernik with lemon, raspberry or orange; the Reine de Saba (all chocolate) and the famous Sachertorte, reinvented by the Boutique Jaune with raspberry.

At the counter they sell traditional gefilte fish (fish balls Jewish style), galeh (calves' feet in jelly), marinated or creamed herring fillets, bobes salad (giant haricot bean salad), Hungarian or Polish goulash, krepleh (big meat raviolis), Russian blinis, Gendarmes (smoked meat sausages), scarlet beef tongue and körözot (paprika cheese from Hungary). You can eat on the spot or take away. All the staff seem to be enjoying themselves and the happy mood is quite infectious.

Address 27 Rue des Rosiers, 75004 Paris, +33 (0)1 42 72 78 91 | **Getting there** Métro to Saint-Paul (Line 1); bus 29, 69, 76 or 96 | **Hours** Wed & Thu 10am–7pm, Fri–Sun 10am–7.30pm | **Tip** At 10 Rue Pavée there is an important synagogue built by the Art Nouveau architect Hector Guimard, who designed the first métro station entrances.

99 __ Schmid

All the flavours of Alsace in the capital

Schmid, the Alsatian food specialists, has been where it is for over a century. But back then when it was established in 1904, the station beside it was called the Gare de Strasbourg, the end of the main line between Paris and Alsace.

Here you can buy all the famous Alsatian specialities: sauerkraut cooked in wine (the Schmid), in champagne (the Royale) or in beer (the Paysanne), quiches, pies, and tarte flambée – the thin Alsatian version of the pizza. At the charcuterie counter they serve the inevitable Frankfurter (pork and veal); the Strasburger (pork and beef); the Gendarmes (pork and beef flavoured with caraway and smoked); smoked pork shoulder, pork knuckle and spare ribs; smoked bacon; black sausage, which you eat cold in slices; and cervelas, which you eat raw in a salad or cooked. On the sweet side, they offer a traditional apple and cinnamon strudel made to reheat at home. And you have the choice between gugelhupf, blueberry or cherry-plum tart. And suspended on freestanding armatures above the counter are Schmid's tasty pretzels, some plain, others with melted cheese.

On the grocery side there are mustards, plain horseradish, rémou-lade or mayonnaise, Christine Ferber's excellent jams, the nonettes of the Maison Lips (round shortbreads made with honey and orange), and the famous Melfor vinegar (flavoured with herbs and honey). The cheese is from Munster, some enhanced with fancy recipes like the Carré Kanzel, matured with cherry-plum schnapps, and the Mini Grès des Vosges, matured with Kirsch.

You can take away or eat on the spot in a very simple environment. The welcome is typically Alsatian, without any fuss, but very convivial. As far as I am concerned, I buy the sauerkraut raw and cook it in my own way – not too much, so it stays a bit crunchy, with the charcuterie of my choice (I prefer it with smoked pork shoulder) – but then I am Alsatian.

Address 76 Boulevard de Strasbourg, 75010 Paris, +33 (0)1 46 07 89 74 | **Getting there** Métro to Gare de l'Est (Line 4); bus 38 | **Hours** Mon–Fri 9am–8pm, Sat 8.30am–7.45pm | **Tip** The Gare de l'Est, which dates back to the middle of the 19th century, is worth visiting. In the middle of the Alsace Hall you can see the plaque marking kilometre zero, the beginning of the Paris–Strasbourg railway line.

100__ Tang Frères

A food empire sprung from an idea

In 1976, two brothers of Chinese Laotian origin took advantage of their country's French-speaking colonial past to create the Company Tang Frères in Paris. Their ambition was to distribute Asian food products throughout the whole of Europe. At first their business was entirely wholesale, but they soon realised the potential of selling directly to the public. They opened their first Asian supermarket in 1981. A few years later they added a traiteur, a grocer and a gourmet caterer. Since then, Tang Frères has become a huge empire with 10 shops, 5 boutique traiteurs, selling more than 11,000 products from over a hundred different countries, the whole enterprise supported by a phenomenal warehouse with 26,000 square metres of storage space.

Their supermarkets abound with the familiar and the rare. Next to flagship products, like the inevitable rice and wheat noodles, coconut milk, fresh meat and poultry, vegetables, herbs, fruit, soya sauces, seasonings, deep-frozen food, sweets and rice vinegars, it is perfectly possible that you will find exactly the little sauce you loved so much during your last trip to Thailand or the aubergine eggplant chutney, which will go perfectly with your next chicken curry. The difficulty is not to buy a lot of tempting products doomed to stay forever as intriguing items on the kitchen shelf. To help you, Tang Frères have printed lots of recipe leaflets that are easy to use. Their shops also sell specialist equipment, like rice-cookers, stacking baskets for dim sum, woks, fondue casseroles, chopsticks and crockery, and the decorative knick-knacks used to dress Oriental tables, all at unbeatable prices.

At Tang Gourmet you can eat on the spot or take away dishes, Vietnamese, Laotian and Chinese specialities, such as Peking duck, the ever-popular Vietnamese bún bò and delicious pork and minced beef sandwiches.

Address 48 Avenue d'Ivry, 75013 Paris (original shop), +33 (0)1 45 70 80 00. Also at 168 Avenue de Choisy, 75013 Paris (Tang Gourmet), +33 (0)1 44 24 06 72 | **Getting there** Métro to Porte d'Ivry (Line 7), or Olympiades (Line 14); bus 62, 64 or 83 | **Hours** Tue–Fri 9am–8pm, Sat 8am–8pm, Sun 8am–1pm | **Tip** The area is full of Chinese and Asian restaurants. It's hard to choose, but try Lao Cai Ragoût at 8 Rue Fragon, or the Paradis Thaï, 132 Rue de Tolbiac.

101__ Télescope
A microscopic focus on exquisite taste

This tiny little café was created in 2012 by Nicolas Clerc and David Flynn. There's little else to look at besides the magnificent Marzocco coffee machine. It serves a straight espresso, a noisette (with a touch of milk giving it a hazelnut colour, hence its name), an allongé, with a little more water, a crème, an au lait, an iced coffee and a tonic coffee (mixed with tonic water, which I found very refreshing). You can also have an intriguing Aeropress – a clever coffee maker invented by an American engineer fed up with not being able to find a machine that made good coffee for one (or at the most two). His method is simple and quick and the result is very near an espresso, though a bit stronger.

You're given the choice between two coffees from Kenya, two from Ethiopia and one from Colombia, a restricted selection in keeping with the minimalist décor. The roasting companies used are the world's best: the English Hasbean, the Norwegian Supreme Roastworks (whose beans you can buy on the spot), the Danish Coffee Collective, the Norwegian Tim Wendelboe and Koppi from Sweden. You can also buy an Aeropress as well as the elegant Chemex cafetière, which makes a very smooth but powerfully aromatic filter coffee.

Télescope also serve teas, hot chocolate and fruit juices. To eat with the drinks, they offer home-made bread with jam, granola with yoghurt, goji berries and fruit, yoghurt with honey and hazelnuts, lemon or chocolate cake, banana loaf, vanilla or olive financiers (little cake-like biscuits that have no name in English), chocolate or caramel cookies, croissant with jam, pain au chocolat, scrambled eggs, egg sandwiches and toast with Comté cheese – everything exquisitely chosen to complement the taste of the drinks.

David has now joined the excellent Brûlerie de Belleville (see ch. 56 and 102), leaving Nicolas to maintain the supreme standards of Télescope.

Address 5 Rue Villedo, 75001 Paris, +33 (0)1 42 61 33 14 | **Getting there** Métro to Pyramides (Line 7 or 14); bus 21, 27, 68, 81 or 95 | **Hours** Mon–Fri 8.30am–5pm, Sat 9.30am–6.30pm | **Tip** In the Basilica of Notre-Dame-des-Victoires you can admire a magnificent array of paintings by Carle Van Loo, first painter to King Louis XV, in the Rococo style.

102__Ten Belles

A peal of bells for brilliant coffee

Thomas Lehoux believes in good coffee. He co-founded the Frog Fight, a competition for the best baristas in Paris – people who specialise in preparing coffee. Then he established La Brûlerie de Belleville with David Flynn – a pioneer coffee house selling only the best coffees from around the world. Now he's opened Ten Belles, named after the famous Ten Bells natural wine bar in New York and an equally well-known pub in London.

Ten Belles is tiny but intense. The dozen tables, with crazy little foldable stools, are shared between the mezzanine, the ground floor and a diminutive terrace in front – all in pure Brooklyn style. All through the day they serve espresso (made in a Marzocco – the Rolls-Royce of coffee machines), a delicious filter coffee, a café latte with an extra-smooth tasting milk foam, a small milk (warm or cold) coffee or an iced latte, and a range of fruit juices. The origins of all the coffees are indicated on the blackboard.

For breakfast, they serve their own Breakfast Bun (ricotta, ham and chives), a Sweet Bun (caramel, chocolate and pistachio) with home-made hot chocolate, a chai latte (tea with spices) or a black, green or spicy tea. For lunch, from 12 o'clock on, they offer a Toastie (feta, spinach, beetroot, almond, parsley and white onions), a Brioche Bun (ham, celery pickles, mayo and salad), two types of focaccias (hummus, beetroot seasoning, sesame seeds, fine herbs and salad, or tuna, mayo, carrot pickles and lemon), a salad (roast chicken, radish, cucumber, capers, celery pickles, lemon and croûtons), and a soup that varies with the season. Anna Trattles' pâtisseries are drop-dead delicious: cookies, scones, brownies, flavoured loaves – perfect for a picnic along the canal.

Thomas has now opened, with friends, Ten Belles Bread on the Rue Bréguet, which sells yeast breads, brioches and focaccias – all home-made.

Address 10 Rue de la Grange aux Belles, 75010 Paris, +33 (0)1 42 40 90 78. Also at 17–19 Rue Bréguet, 75011 Paris | **Getting there** Métro to Jacques Bonsergent (Line 5); bus 46 or 75 | **Hours** Mon–Fri 8am–5pm, Sat & Sun 9am–6pm | **Tip** Across the Grange-aux-Belles bridge you'll find the Hôtel du Nord, which gave its name to the famous film by Marcel Carné with Arletty and Louis Jouvet.

103__ Terra Corsa

Grown-up tastes from the Island of Beauty

Corsica is France's largest island and the birthplace of Napoleon. The French call it the *Île de Beauté* (Island of Beauty) because of its dramatic Mediterranean landscape, but it's famous, too, for its food. The hot climate and special vegetation produce distinctive strong tastes, which can all be enjoyed at Terra Corsa, where everything is Corsican.

On entering the shop, one's eye is immediately caught by the variety of saucissons and hams hanging from the ceiling: lonzu (dried pork fillet), figatellu (made with pork liver, which explains its dark colour), coppa (salted and dried pork neck), pancetta (salted and dried pork belly) and prizuttu (dried ham). All these products come from traditional local producers. Corsican pork saucisson is made from wild pigs, which roam freely in the forests, feeding on chestnuts and acorns. This can make supplies a bit unpredictable. Corsican cheeses are well represented, like brocciu, tomme and Fium'Orbo – which is rather strong and which you eat with fig jam. The Corsicans like to say that cheese is milk turning into an adult. Everything here has a grown-up taste.

Corsican wines are well represented, such as Patrimonio, Sartène and Cap Corse, as well as beers and liquors. Plus, of course, olive oil. There's also Corsican coke, Corsican water, Corsican fruit juices, terrines, jams (fig and tangerine) and chutneys. Among the sweet offerings are the famous Canistrelli – dried almond biscuits with a lemon or aniseed flavour – and Fiadone – a lemon-flavoured flan.

At the tables, you can eat quiche with a salad, charcuterie, or cheese board, or mixed board with terrine, with, of course, a fine glass of Corsican wine. Terra Corsa also offers sandwiches. I tried the dried ham, olive oil, sheep tomme and sun-dried tomatoes – great! The little terrace at the back, in the peaceful tree-lined Cours des Petites-Écuries, is a quiet heaven in a very busy street.

Address 61 bis Rue du Faubourg Saint-Denis, 75010 Paris, +33 (0)1 45 23 18 94 |
Getting there Métro to Château d'Eau (Line 4); bus 35, 38, 39, 46 or 65 | **Hours** Daily
10am–11pm | **Tip** The Cour des Petites-Écuries is a harbour of peace, with beautiful
restaurants and street lamps.

104__ La Tête Dans Les Olives

Ancient farm tastes of Sicily brought to the city

As soon as you enter this little shop you feel the presence of a personal passion. Just by the entrance are a few fresh products, always seasonal. I saw little pears and tomatoes, all from Sicily. The shop's founder, Cédric Casanova's mother is French but his father is Sicilian, and his affection for this island springs from the holidays he spent there as a child. One day, when returning from a holiday in Sicily, he brought back 100 litres of olive oil, which he sold to friends in 4 days. This was how the idea for importing Sicilian olive oil was born. He opened his shop, La Tête Dans les Olives, in 2007.

Traditionally, olive oil in Sicily was not made to be sold but produced solely for family needs. For this reason, ancient means of production survived: oil made in small batches from individual, often very old olive orchards. Casanova identified the distinct tastes of all these different oils, which can vary even though the fields are only 100 yards apart. The 40–50 oils he makes every year are always single varieties from specific localities, avoiding any blends. These oils fill one wall of his shop, many in large metal containers with taps so you can buy as little or as much as you like, others in individual cans and bottles, all very soberly but elegantly designed. La Table Unique in the middle of the shop provides a place for tasting, but for six people only, by reservation.

The shop also offers choice delicacies from Sicily, many made to Casanova's recipes, such as the exceptional Passulune olives, gathered from a very late harvest, anchovy fillets and pasta, onion jam, pickled caper leaves, flavoured salts, tomato or basil pesto, tuna in olive oil, dried basil flowers to add a special taste to a salad, dried nettle leaves to make infusions, the 'little ring' pasta Primeluci made by the Gallo brothers, whole tomatoes, bottled or in sauces, and honeys.

Address 2 Rue Sainte-Marthe, 75010 Paris, +33 (0)9 51 31 33 34. Also at 54 Rue du Couëdic, 75014 Paris | **Getting there** Métro to Goncourt (Line 3); bus 46 or 75 | **Hours** Tue 11am – 1pm & 2 – 7pm, Wed – Sat 10am – 1pm & 2 – 7pm | **Tip** The area is one of the old working-class districts in Paris, with many old properties – just stroll around and discover. There is almost a Neapolitan atmosphere.

105 _ Trois Fois Plus de Piment
Some like it hot

There's a little room downstairs and another on the mezzanine, linked by a tiny spiral staircase. You perch on stools or benches at wooden tables, surrounded by entertaining bric-a-brac. The staff are 100 per cent Chinese. In the kitchen, they're all men – only five in a tiny space; outside it's almost all women wearing attractive aprons with leather straps. Orders are taken on tablets, and go direct to the kitchen. Everyone is extremely friendly and impeccably efficient.

The cuisine is from Szechuan and it's absolutely delicious: pork raviolis with Szechuan sauce; beef noodle soup with bamboo shoots; Chinese cabbage and herbs in a pork stock; vermicelli soup with sweet potato vermicelli, celeriac, soya shoots, herbs, peanuts, crushed pimento and pork stock; home-made dandan noodles, minced pork, peanuts, Chinese cabbage, herbs, garlic and pork stock; pork raviolis with or without pimento soup; home-made noodles with minced pork, Chinese cabbage and herbs; vegetarian noodle soup. With or without soup is optional for most dishes. And when they take the order they ask how hot you like your dish, i.e. which level of spice you want, between one and five (five is too hot even for Marilyn). There's a veritable ballet of service between the cooks, the waiters, the customers, the people waiting for takeaways (about 10 minutes max.) and expectant delivery staff. Everything is performed at breakneck speed, as if it's too hot to handle. On the door a small note warns you, without embarrassment, to take care because 'spicy food can cause little (or big) undesirable intestinal derangement'!

If you want a slightly more peaceful environment, visit their sister restaurant Cinq Fois Plus de Piment (along the road at 170 Rue Saint-Martin), which serves baos (little stuffed dumplings steam cooked or grilled) in a much cooler setting. And the queue there is usually much shorter.

Address 184 Rue Saint-Martin, 75003 Paris, +33 (0)6 52 66 75 31 | **Getting there** Métro to Rambuteau (Line 11); bus 29, 38, 47 or 75 | **Hours** Tue–Sat noon–3pm & 7–11pm, Sun noon–3pm & 6.45–11pm | **Tip** At 157 Rue Saint-Martin, La Maison de la Poésie, in the Théâtre Molière, presents readings of contemporary poetry.

106__ Urfa Dürüm

The best kebab in a modest corner

Forget everything you thought you knew about kebabs – the identikit banal mouthful, with chips and mayonnaise, tasting a bit like engine grease. This little place, owned by a Kurdish family, is something else, and great. The father, a political refugee, first arrived in France in 1993, followed by his family, and then opened this kebab shop in 2007.

They warn you at the entrance that their meat is not halal. The menu is very short – kebabs with minced meat, either lamb or free-range chicken or lamb's liver (I didn't have the guts to try this). There's a vegetarian option and a lahmacun (a leaner version of the full kebab – a parcel of thin bread, herbs with minced meat, tomatoes, red onions, rocket or salad and lemon juice – delicious!).

The word *dürüm* means 'wrapped' in Turkish, and that's what you watch as you queue. The galettes (flat breads) are kneaded, flattened and cooked on the spot before your eyes. The boss takes your order and transmits it to his nephew working at the big grill where the meat skewers are cooking. He uses a simple hairdryer to keep the embers glowing, adding a touch of folk humour to the whole performance. Then all the ingredients are neatly rolled, at lightning speed, in a galette, hot from the oven, and your kebab is ready to eat on the spot, on the little stools inside and outside, or to take away. There's no oozing sauce, no dripping grease. Everything is, and tastes, absolutely fresh. It's hardly surprising that the queue never stops.

To drink you have a choice between their Dew (also called ayran) – a home-made beverage of curdled milk, salted and lemon flavoured – beer or Kurdish wine. On the wall, a few posters proclaim the struggles of the Kurdish people. Everyone is really nice even when, as usual, it's packed. You could easily walk past this little place without noticing it, but don't miss it. It's a special and unexpected treat in the French capital.

Address 58 Rue du Faubourg Saint-Denis, 75010 Paris, +33 (0)1 48 24 12 84 | **Getting there** Métro to Château d'Eau (Line 4); bus 35, 38, 39, 46, 56 or 65 | **Hours** Weekdays 11.30am–midnight, Sun 11.30am–10pm | **Tip** La Gare de l'Est, in the Place du 11 Novembre 1918, is a classified historic monument with its paintings celebrating the heroes of World War I.

107__Le Verre Volé Belleville
A treasure trove of France and Europe's best

This grocery store is a mine of good things: oils from La Tête dans les Olives (see ch. 104) and Jocelyn in Ardèche, canned products by Anne Rozès (pork paté, the best black sausage, cassoulet, Basque piperade and rillettes), grilled peppers from Primavera, monkfish liver from Petit Prince, the mustards and gherkins of Edmond Fallot, cooked ham from the Ferme de Mayrinhac, Spanish tuna belly, tuna and mackerel rillettes, sun-dried tomatoes, spices from the Saveurs du Cachemire, Martelli pastas, fruit juices by Patrick Font, Elixia artisanal lemonade, Bordier yoghurt, the mozzarella of Nanina (see ch. 76), raw milk cheeses, artisanal charcuteries such as Spanish Bellota chorizo, Bellota black pudding and fresh sausages from Mayrinhac, dry ham from Auvergne and Parma, fresh eggs from Perche, salt flakes from Maldon in England… and a few sweets such as le Bonbon Français, flavoured naturally, without chemicals. You can, by the way, also find them at La Maison Plisson (see ch. 67) and La Grande Épicerie (see ch. 49). In the cellar, they stock only natural wine.

The sandwiches are top class, based on the traditional baguette: charcuterie or cheese, charcuterie and cheese, croque-monsieur made with Morbier cheese, lamb merguez with mint cream / grilled courgettes, scrambled eggs / guindillas (little sweet pimentos) and manchego cheese. The fillings change according to the season and the inspiration of the day. For dessert, they serve Terre Adélice's delicious organic ice creams. You can eat at the small number of tables inside and the service is welcoming and efficient.

Round the corner, at 38 Rue de Oberkampf, the Verre Volé wine cellar stocks all the natural wines you could possibly wish for, with the slight drawback that, when I was there, the service left a lot to be desired. But I can recommend, most warmly, the Verre Volé at 67 Rue de Lancry 75010, with both a wine cellar and an excellent restaurant.

Address 54 Rue de la Folie Méricourt, 75011 Paris, +33 (0)1 48 05 36 55 | **Getting there** Métro to Saint-Ambroise (Line 9) or Richard-Lenoir (Line 5); bus 56 or 96 | **Hours** Mon–Sat 10.30am–8pm | **Tip** The Rue Oberkampf shelters two remarkable cul-de-sacs: la Cité du Figuier at no. 104–106 and the Cité Durmar at no. 154, an old market garden flanked by little studio homes.

108__ Wild & the Moon
The organic Starbucks of the future

Wild & the Moon has a simple but bold ambition: to let you enjoy eating to the full, while doing good to yourself and the planet. Emmanuelle and Hervé Sawko, together with Gregory Khellouf, created the concept of Wild & the Moon in 2016. They established their first Parisian shop in the trendy Rue Charlot, with the ambition of becoming the organic Starbucks. At Wild & the Moon nothing is hidden; everything is on display, following their belief in absolute transparency. All produce is precisely labelled and the food is prepared in front of the clients, with complete descriptions given of all the meals you can eat on the spot or take away.

The dishes on offer are prodigious, each named to catch the mood of the moment: the Power Bowl (almonds, spirulina, banana, apple lemon and linseed), the Açai Bowl (açai berries mixed with home-made granola, coconut flakes and fresh banana) and the Nice Cream Bowl (fresh coconut flesh, coconut milk, puffed quinoa and goji berries). They also offer really rich Super Bowls, such as the Green Bowl (avocado, broccoli, cucumber, kohlrabi, wild greens, lamb's lettuce, hemp seeds, vegan cheese with cumin and spirulina sauce). Their desserts are equally imaginative, like the Wild Muesli (gluten-free oats, almond milk, raisins, chia seeds, apples, goji berries, pumpkin seeds and maple syrup) or the Strawberry Coco Latte (coconut yoghurt, cashew nuts, lemon, almonds, maple syrup, with a strawberry coulis). Among the hot beverages are the Charcoal Latte (almond milk, maple syrup, charcoal, rice bran, vanilla and coconut milk) and the Mocha (espresso, almond milk, raw chocolate and vanilla). For cold drinks they offer the Coco Crush (non-pasteurised coconut water and chia seeds) and the Liquid Vitality (lemon, ginger, cider vinegar and maple syrup). The fruit juices are cold pressed and, of course, 100 per cent absolutely natural.

Address 55 Rue Charlot, 75003 Paris, +33 (0)1 86 95 40 46 | **Getting there** Métro to Filles du Calvaire (Line 8); bus 29, 75 or 96 | **Hours** Mon–Fri 8am–10.30pm, Sat & Sun 9am–10.30pm | **Tip** On International Women's Day, on 8 March, 2007, the crossing between the Rue de Turenne, Rue Charlot and Rue de Franche-Comté was renamed Place Olympe-de-Gouges, in honour of one of the great early campaigners for equal rights for women.

109__ Workshop Isse
The flavours of Japan in the heart of Paris

Walking into Workshop Isse transports you into a shop in a back-street of Tokyo or Kyoto, not sophisticatedly designed, but a jumble, though naturally elegant, of all things Japanese. Customers sit at tables or at the counter, eating and drinking among the heaving shelves of produce. Workshop is a good name for the place, because one feels here that you can try everything.

Toshiro Kuroda arrived in Paris in the 1970s, working first in journalism. Then, in 2004, he opened Workshop Isse in Paris' Little Tokyo. He imported the best Japanese products made without additives by small artisan producers: spices, condiments, seaweeds, tea, rice, noodles and sakes. If you hesitate between the bewildering variety of soya, dashi or ponzu sauces on offer, smiling and attentive staff will let you taste them. The only problem is that they're all delicious! But the relaxed, unhurried ambiance of the place gives one the peace to make up one's mind.

Workshop Isse is more than just a shop. It's a perfect stopping-off place for lunch. You have to eat what they're making and they change it every day, which tempts you back and back. For €15 you can taste four delicious dishes with a bowl of sticky rice. We had green beans with soya sauce and crushed sesame, a dish of burdock, lotus, carrots and shitake mushrooms, another of chicken in a stock of miso soup (fermented soya beans) made with sake lees (yeast residue) and, finally, marinated salmon in a mix of mirin (a sweet rice wine) and rice vinegar, yuzu juice (a kind of lemon) and soya sauce. Pudding, sake and tea are a little extra.

They have another shop on the opposite side of the street – a beautiful place decorated with ceramics and sake barrels where they organise sake tastings, accompanied, of course, with tasty titbits. If you want to find out about Japanese food, Workshop Isse is where to begin, and end.

Address 11 Rue Saint-Augustin, 75002 Paris, +33 (0)1 42 96 26 74 | **Getting there**
Métro to Quatre-Septembre (Line 3); bus 21, 27, 29, 39, 68, 81 or 95 | **Hours** Mon–Sat
11am–7.30pm | **Tip** At no. 23 is the entrance to the Galerie Vivienne, one of the
grandest arcades in Paris and now a historic monument. Its décor, which is neoclassical
in style, is ornamented with mosaics and sculptures in praise of trade. It leads to the
beautiful Galerie Colbert.

110_ Yann Couvreur Pâtisserie
The art of pastry for everyone

Yann Couvreur first worked in the Prince de Galles, Park Hyatt and Burgundy Palace hotels. But he wanted a place where he could give his artistic and culinary talents free rein and share his creations directly with the public. So he left the exclusive world of upmarket hotels and opened his first shop in the Avenue Parmentier, in a busy and popular quarter of Paris. There, anyone, not just the rich, could come in off the street and enjoy breakfast or lunch or just a single pastry with a cup of coffee.

Success led him to open a second shop, a tearoom in the Rue des Rosiers where you can find all his now famous pâtisseries: the raspberry and mint baba, the lime tart with a meringue topping, his amazing rectangular éclairs, with chocolate, tonka bean, or milk chocolate with coconut and his basil and strawberry tart.

Yann Couvreur's signature pâtisserie is without question his mille-feuille. It's made of arlettes (fine, brittle tiles) of kouign amann (a traditional pastry from Britanny made with buckwheat flour) with whipped cream and Madagascar vanilla. The confection, which rises in a minute, is ephemeral but unforgettable. But beware, they can only make a limited edition of 50 in a day, so you have to get there early.

At his savoury counter, Yann Couvreur offers sandwiches (roast chicken, tarragon pesto, dried tomato preserved in olive oil), quiches (organic vegetable and goat's cheese) and feuilletés (sandwiches of puff pastry – I tried the salmon one, a perfect balance of tastes in the mouth). All these delicacies are made in long strips and sold in five-centimetre blocks. You can taste them on the spot with a coffee, tea or fruit juice, or take away. Sunday brunch is served, offering yoghurt with granola, tiramisu and panna cotta. Yann Couvreur grew up in Velizy, on the edge of the forest, and loves foxes, which explains his company's symbol.

Address 137 Avenue Parmentier, 75010 Paris, +33 (0)1 42 45 71 35. Also at 23 Rue des Rosiers, 75004 Paris and YC Espace Café, Galeries Lafayette | Getting there Métro to Goncourt (Line 11); bus 46 or 75 | Hours Daily 8am–8pm | Tip The superb entrance to Métro Parmentier, in front of no. 88, was designed in 1900 by Hector Guimard and is now a classified historic monument.

111 Yves-Marie Le Bourdonnec

Where meat tastes of meat

Like Hugo Desnoyer, Yves-Marie Le Bourdonnec is a butcher who loves animals and works closely with the farmers who breed them. He started work as a butcher when he was in his teens, and his passion for his trade has grown with the years (his two sons now work with him). It's hardly surprising that he's been named Best Butcher in Paris. Nevertheless, he prefers British cattle, in particular the famous Black Angus, and advocates crossing this breed with French animals.

All his meat is most carefully selected and prepared. His prime rib beef is matured for 60 days. His lamb is reared on salt marshes near the sea. His pork is Black Bigorre, matured for 10 days. His hens, from the Perche region, are 'poularde', that is they are kept from cocks and don't lay eggs, but instead grow deliciously plump. He also stocks world rarities like Wagyu beef, from Japan, and a Spanish breed of cow, the Galician Red, which is matured between 80 and 100 days. And there is his own Salaté Le Bourdonnec, which is a shoulder of beef rubbed with garlic, marinated in salt and totally wrapped in aromatic herbs and then encased in hay.

His home-made preparations include lamb chops in pesto, a gigot cooked very slowly over a long time with Lardo di Colonnata, garlic and thyme, and his poularde cooked in a clay shell with aromatic herbs, Lardo di Colonnata and figs. His charcuteries are superb: chipolatas, herb sausage, raw ham and salamis. Naturally, not everything is available all through the year, so for special orders it's wise to phone in advance. Le Bourdonnec has now opened a restaurant at Gourmet La Fayette, which offers his steak of the day, T-bone or matured beef rib. He developed a special blend of beef for burgers that you can taste at Blend, which has several addresses in Paris, a recipe selected for special mention by *The New York Times*.

Address 43 Rue du Cherche-Midi, 75006 Paris, +33 (0)1 42 22 35 52. Also at 172 Avenue Victor Hugo, 75016 Paris and 25 Rue Ramey, 75018 Paris (Timothée Sautereau) | **Getting there** Métro to Saint-Placide (Line 4) or Sèvres-Babylone (Line 10 or 12); bus 39 or 70 | **Hours** Tue–Sat 9am–1pm, 3.30–7.30pm | **Tip** The nearby Rue du Regard contains several beautiful Parisian town houses that have been listed as historic monuments. See how rich Parisians used to live.

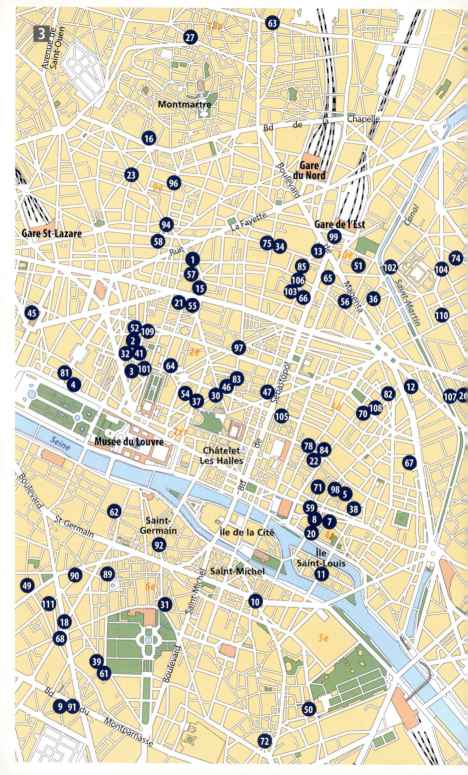

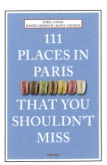

Sybil Canac, Renée Grimaud,
Katia Thomas
**111 Places in Paris
That You Shouldn't Miss**
ISBN 978-3-7408-0159-5

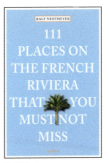

Ralf Nestmeyer
**111 Places on the French Riviera
That You Must Not Miss**
ISBN 978-3-95451-612-4

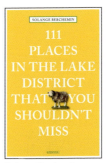

Solange Berchemin
**111 Places in the Lake District
That You Shouldn't Miss**
ISBN 978-3-7408-0378-0

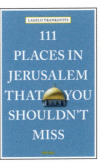

Laszlo Trankovits
**111 Places in Jerusalem
That You Shouldn't Miss**
ISBN 978-3-7408-0320-9

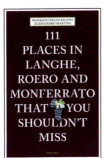

Maurizio Francesconi,
Alessandro Martini
**111 Places in Langhe, Roero and
Monferrato That You Shouldn't Miss**
ISBN 978-3-7408-0399-5

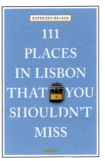

Kathleen Becker
**111 Places in Lisbon
That You Shouldn't Miss**
ISBN 978-3-7408-0383-4

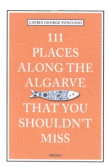

Catrin George Ponciano
111 Places along the Algarve
That You Shouldn't Miss
ISBN 978-3-7408-0381-0

Alexia Amvrazi, Diana Farr Louis,
Diane Shugart, Yannis Varouhakis
111 Places in Athens
That You Shouldn't Miss
ISBN 978-3-7408-0377-3

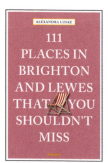

Alexandra Loske
111 Places in Brighton and Lewes
That You Shouldn't Miss
ISBN 978-3-7408-0255-4

Fabrizio Ardito
111 Places in Malta
That You Shouldn't Miss
ISBN 978-3-7408-0261-5

Tom Shields, Gillian Tait
111 Places in Glasgow
That You Shouldn't Miss
ISBN 978-3-7408-0256-1

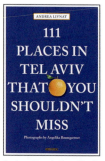

Andrea Livnat, Angelika Baumgartner
111 Places in Tel Aviv
That You Shouldn't Miss
ISBN 978-3-7408-0263-9

Kay Walter, Rüdiger Liedtke
111 Places in Brussels
That You Shouldn't Miss
ISBN 978-3-7408-0259-2

Kai Oidtmann
111 Places in Iceland
That You Shouldn't Miss
ISBN 978-3-7408-0030-7

Thomas Fuchs
111 Places in Amsterdam
That You Shouldn't Miss
ISBN 978-3-7408-0023-9

Michael Glover, Richard Anderson
111 Places in Sheffield
That You Shouldn't Miss
ISBN 978-3-7408-0022-2

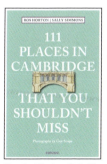

Rosalind Horton, Sally Simmons,
Guy Snape
111 Places in Cambridge
That You Shouldn't Miss
ISBN 978-3-7408-0147-2

Justin Postlethwaite
111 Places in Bath
That You Shouldn't Miss
ISBN 978-3-7408-0146-5

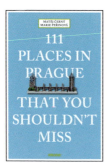

Matěj Černý, Marie Peřinová
111 Places in Prague
That You Shouldn't Miss
ISBN 978-3-7408-0144-1

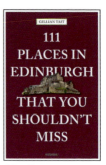

Gillian Tait
111 Places in Edinburgh
That You Shouldn't Miss
ISBN 978-3-95451-883-8

Julian Treuherz, Peter de Figueiredo
111 Places in Liverpool
That You Shouldn't Miss
ISBN 978-3-95451-769-5

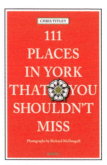

Chris Titley
111 Places in York
That You Shouldn't Miss
ISBN 978-3-95451-768-8

Frank McNally
111 Places in Dublin
That You Must Not Miss
ISBN 978-3-95451-649-0

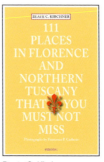

Beate C. Kirchner
111 Places in Florence and Northern
Tuscany That You Must Not Miss
ISBN 978-3-95451-613-1

Giulia Castelli Gattinara,
Mario Verin
111 Places in Milan
That You Must Not Miss
ISBN 978-3-95451-331-4

Petra Sophia Zimmermann
111 Places in Verona
and Lake Garda
That You Must Not Miss
ISBN 978-3-95451-611-7

John Sykes, Birgit Weber
111 Places in London
That You Shouldn't Miss
ISBN 978-3-95451-346-8

Marcus X. Schmid
111 Places in Istanbul
That You Must Not Miss
ISBN 978-3-95451-423-6

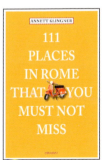

Annett Klingner
111 Places in Rome
That You Must Not Miss
ISBN 978-3-95451-469-4

Rüdiger Liedtke
111 Places in Mallorca
That You Shouldn't Miss
ISBN 978-3-95451-281-2

Acknowledgements

This book has been a big undertaking and has depended on the help of many friends and acquaintances, not to mention the people in the venues, who have been extremely helpful.

But I would like to thank specially Marianne and François Niney, Babeth and Christian Grosrichard, Philippe Vaures and Caroline Wetzel, Sophie Lynch and of course David Valy, who was a fount of information.

The author

Irène Lassus-Fuchs is a restaurateur, cook and translator who has lived and worked in Paris for nearly 40 years. She opened the highly successful Les Petites Sorcières restaurant in Rue Liancourt in the 14th Arrondissement in 1982, and has since established new restaurants in Paris, Strasbourg and Marseille. Her translations include many British and American cook books on cuisine from all over the world, including several books on the crafts, history of art, architecture and design. She now specialises in event catering.

The photographer

Julian Spalding is a writer and former museum director for the cities of Sheffield, Manchester and Glasgow. He established the Ruskin Gallery, the St Mungo Museum of Religious Art and Life and Glasgow's Gallery of Modern Art. His several books include *The Art of Wonder* (which won the Sir Bannister Fletcher Prize for the best art book in 2006), Realisation – from Seeing to Understanding and the e-pamphlet Con Art – why you should sell your Damien Hirst while you can. He has broadcast frequently on BBC radio and TV. Julian lives in Paris.